Praise for *Where Do I Go from Here?*

So many widows have told me just how helpful Miriam has been to them in their unwanted journey as a widow. In her first book and on her website she gives so many practical helps—but now, with *Where Do I Go from Here?* she becomes more philosophical. The truths, which she illustrates with riveting stories, equipped Miriam to have a rich life ministering to widows in Africa and around the world. Your life is not over—it has taken a sharp turn, but it can still be full and meaningful. Miriam will help you again.

> —**DEE BRESTIN**, author of *The God of All Comfort* and
> *The Friendships of Women*

A big thanks to Miriam Neff for her encouragement to those who have suffered significant loss. She nudges us to beyond our tendency to stare into the rearview mirror and moves us forward to all that God has for us in the future. Her helpful insights are grounded in her own journey, which validates the principles that she shares in this important book.

> —**JOSEPH M. STOWELL**, president, Cornerstone University,
> Grand Rapids, Michigan

WHERE DO I GO FROM HERE?

Bold Living after Unwanted Change

MIRIAM NEFF

MOODY PUBLISHERS
CHICAGO

All Scripture quotations, unless otherwise indicated, are taken from the *Holy Bible, New International Version*®, NIV®. Copyright ©1973, 1978, 1984, 2011 by Biblica, Inc.™ Used by permission of Zondervan. All rights reserved worldwide. www.zondervan.com.

Scripture quotations marked NKJV are taken from the *New King James Version*. Copyright © 1982 by Thomas Nelson, Inc. Used by permission. All rights reserved.

Scripture quotations marked NLT are taken from the *Holy Bible, New Living Translation*, copyright © 1996, 2004. Used by permission of Tyndale House Publishers, Inc., Wheaton Illinois 60189, U.S.A. All rights reserved.

Scripture quotations marked ASV are taken from the *American Standard Version*, 1901, copyright expired, public domain.

Edited by Annette LaPlaca
Interior design: Ragont Design
Cover design: Barb Fisher / LeVan Fisher Design
Cover image: iStock / John Woodcock
Author photo: Jim Whitmer

Library of Congress Cataloging-in-Publication Data

Neff, Miriam.
    Where do I go from here? : bold living after unwanted change / Miriam Neff.
        p. cm.
    Includes bibliographical references (p.   ).
    ISBN 978-0-8024-0449-7
    1. Life change events—Religious aspects—Christianity. 2. Loss (Psychology)—Religious aspects—Christianity. 3. Adjustment (Psychology)—Religious aspects—Christianity. 4. Change—Religious aspects—Christianity. I. Title.
BV4509.5.N44 2012
248.8'6--dc23

                                                                    2012010821

All websites and phone numbers listed herein are accurate at the time of publication, but may change in the future or cease to exist. The listing of website references and resources does not imply publisher endorsement of the site's entire contents. Groups and organizations are listed for informational purposes, and listing does not imply publisher endorsement of their activities.

For Edward, Albert, and Edmond Hogan,
Living boldly, inspiring, affirming, and proving
that overcoming is ever possible, regardless of the past.
You are my heroes.
Love, Nana

Contents

Foreword

I had the pleasure of meeting Miriam Neff more than two years ago through a mutual friend. Miriam and I were having dinner on a warm summer evening in the suburbs of Chicago, sharing our stories and getting to know one another as we discussed the possibility of her teaching in our fall grief support workshop at Willow Creek Community Church. Miriam showed the qualities I look for in all of our teachers: compassion, empathy, and hard-won wisdom learned from surviving and successfully coming out the other side of a grief journey. But her ability to talk about losing her beloved husband while projecting joy, comfort, and a love of life was both fascinating and comforting. While listening to Miriam's story, I could immediately tell that she "got it." She was part of a club—a club no one would ever willingly choose to join—of those left behind to cope with life after death.

There is nothing we experience that knocks us off our feet like losing someone we love. There is nothing in this life that prepares us for the shock of the end. And when that happens, we frantically look around for something to hang on to—for something that can guide us through this difficult and unknown territory.

I read Miriam's first book on becoming a widow, *From One Widow to Another*. Then, when I heard her teach, I saw close-up how my workshop participants connected with her honesty, her practicality, and the hope that radiated from her grace-filled presentation. They also knew that she "got it"—that she was one of them—and they could trust her advice, her wisdom, and the God-grounded healing process she teaches. Miriam's knowledge and wisdom encompassed more than understanding what it meant to be a widow; she really understood how to rebuild a life after a major loss. I encouraged Miriam to view her experience through the wider lens of coming to terms with loss and tragedy. I felt strongly that her advice could be applied across a broader category of individuals coping with many kinds of grief.

I see a spiritual electricity working through Miriam's life as she courageously shares her deep well of knowledge and love with those seeking to create a new life with hope and a future. Thank you, Miriam, for obeying God's call on your life and experience.

NANCY HAMLIN
Grief Support Workshop Leader and Teacher
Willow Creek Community Church

Introduction:
Tilt the Kaleidoscope

You've lost someone or something precious. That's why you picked up this book. There's little comfort in knowing that no human avoids loss in this life. The fact that change happens and rarely is all-positive doesn't soothe your soul. Your heart cries out that you're alone, you're isolated, and no one understands. Your mind struggles to wrap around the unthinkable: *This tragedy happens to others, not me!* Your soul shrivels and suggests that shrinking and hibernation are options.

I can assure you that we were not intended to embrace loss. Loss of any important relationship; divorce; home foreclosure; bankruptcy; death of your child, your soul-mate sister, or spouse; incarceration, suicide, disability, career implosions—these were not part of our Creator's original plan.

Yet the instinct of your heart, mind, and soul might be right. Things might get worse. Your loss *could* be followed by more bad stuff. Japan's tragic earthquake created a tsunami and was followed by more destruction as power plants overheated and tremors continued to cause more damage. Seldom is loss a single event. Whether in tiny ripples or larger waves, touching relationships and the rhythm of our daily routine, loss impacts our total being. While denial and disbelief might be tempting, those responses don't calm the real ripples and waves in our season of loss.

 We were not intended to embrace loss. Loss was not part of our Creator's original plan.

Isolation, disbelief, and hibernating may look like your only options with no end in sight. But before you settle in there, take the chance to explore with me in this book some other possibilities.

I cannot tell you I understand your loss because I don't. My greatest loss, that of losing my soul-mate husband and best friend to a terrible disease, does not allow me to step into your shoes—nor does the reality that someone I loved dearly was incarcerated or that I'm estranged from a relative who never wants to see me again. I have lived my own losses, but I have not lived *your* loss. No one has. But there are common threads that connect us through the emotions we all share. We're stronger if we share them. We *do* share the possibility of the loss taking us further down *or* the possibility of that loss becoming the catalyst for a new beginning we'd never dreamed of. I'm not exaggerating, my friend. You may not see this now, but sharing what we have in common is vital. I know good new things are possible because I'm living it.

Life is like a kaleidoscope. We point our cylinder toward the light, peer in, and see a beautiful array of glass and stones reflecting beauty, diversity, and contrast. We adjust the lens, and another beautiful, yet different combination of color evolves. Then suddenly the kaleidoscope is thrust to face a black hole. No light means no beautiful display.

When you timidly, maybe fearfully, tilt your kaleidoscope back toward the light, you'll see a new combination you've never seen before, colors you didn't know existed. Location and contrast create new and unexpected beauty.

May I share just one example from my new life? I traveled the world with my husband, Bob. We didn't trudge through forty-plus countries—we joyfully trotted. He was helping fledgling broadcasters. I was delighted to be part of the journey. When Bob exited to heaven, I grieved many huge and important losses. One small loss was grieving traveling the world. I had loved it! When I met Bob as a college freshman on Indiana University's campus, he asked me what I wanted to do after I graduated. I told him, "Travel the world." I married him at age nineteen and traveled to Chicago. But my dream for world travel eventually happened. But with the loss of Bob, it was over!

My kaleidoscope was pointing into a black hole. As I looked around for help, I came to realize that the resources I needed to exit the black hole of widowhood did not exist. Eventually I realized that I should create resources for the benefit of the next person. Widow Connection, Inc., became a website, a book, a media outlet, and more. We knew we wanted to reach farther, become more global in helping widows. I'd seen young widows in Africa. Their haunting eyes, thin bodies, and stooped shoulders shouted, "Empty!" Yet they bore the weight and responsibility of their dependent children.

The result? I'm traveling again. To Africa! We're helping those young widows learn the skill of sewing. Every year we've begun a new project. And those opportunities may increase! Lest you think I'm living in a dream world, happily-ever-after with a beautiful mission in place of my awesome man, let me give you a glimpse of my first trip.

After a week in Malawi, I traveled alone to Maputo, Mozambique. The plan: to start a sewing project for the widows in the Mukhotweni village. Having communicated the plan, sent money ahead to purchase the machines, and emailed my contact my arrival information, I landed at the hot noon hour with great anticipation.

No one held up a cardboard sign reading "Neff." No problem, I'd just wait—hour after hour after hour. Developing-world airports are different from the ones Americans are used to. There were no benches, but a crumbling curb outside would do. I had no phone contact numbers, nor an address for where I'd be staying that night. Aggressive young men pressed me, asking to carry my luggage. Taxi drivers urged me to climb in. I don't speak Portuguese. How do you sign, "I don't know where I'm going"? One young man wore a white shirt and black trousers, which made him stand out in the crowd. His sign bore the name of a hotel. He approached me politely, speaking some English. I explained my dilemma. We trooped inside to the phone books where he searched for the organization my contact represented. It existed! But no one answered the office phone. Saturday afternoon would soon be Saturday evening. My choices were narrowing.

 I know good new things are possible because I'm living it.

I returned to my curbside seat and waited. Finally I asked him what the cost would be for a taxi to that address. *Good to know,* I thought. Another hour passed. Bob always said my mental computer had no fear chip. Lucky thing! Dusk was approaching, and I was the only woman in sight. The polite young hotel driver finally approached me and explained that it was time for him to go off-duty and I should not stay there alone. He would take me to that address. I scrambled gladly into his taxi.

The adventure did not end there. But I'm here to write about it. Broken machines, outside "plumbing" to be visited in complete blackness of night, a sewing trainer who slept during class, heat in my hut that tempted me to throw off the mosquito net for a bit of moving air—it was a harsh beginning. And yet I treasure the courageous widows I met. For every week I give Africa, Africa takes another chunk of my heart. And this is just one piece of my new beginning.

So, you see, I'm not just trying to wrap words around a theory that might be helpful to you. I've lived some losses and can promise you that good things can be ahead. I will not tell you that you can return to the life you had before your loss, or that it will be a smooth road forward. But as I gently tell you, "You can't have your old life back," I'll share how some of us have tilted our kaleidoscope toward the light. The biggest losers can become winners. Yes, we have a void that screams to be filled. Another word for temptation to fill that void is *opportunity*. And opportunity is the birthplace of innovation.

Clayton Christensen beat heart attack, advanced stage cancer, and stroke—all in three years. And he coined a new phrase: "disruptive innovation." He was describing business solutions in which new simple technologies and inventions bring down big companies because what the big companies do is no longer needed. He related this to innovations in the health care field. Other examples are cell phones making landline phones unnecessary and scanners replacing Xerox machines. Disruption is not without pain, but disruption is usually necessary for innovation.

The concept has an application to our lives after loss and tragedy. We can discover simpler, unexpected solutions to the new challenges in our lives. The void can be filled with what we might not have imagined before. Our loss has been disruptive, without a doubt. But innovation would never have happened otherwise.

When I was traveling with Bob, we were always met at airports and most of our plans materialized as expected. That did not happen with my first sewing project trip. Some situations were not safe. I imagine that by the time I arrived back in Chicago, my guardian angel (if we have them, and I hope we do) made an appointment with the powers in heaven. I imagine that with tattered, grey feathers, fatigue, and frustration resulting from 24/7 service required to look after me, that poor angel must have begged for a different assignment. The angel might have found it fun when I learned to sail a catamaran solo on the ocean. The guardian angel was probably finding it harder to keep me from careening into trees on my first adventure skiing down the icy mountain slopes in New Hampshire. But this Africa thing? Enough already! That poor angel! Innovations are a part of my new life.

We are not forced to embrace opportunity. We can stagnate and not allow our minds room to explore new beginnings. We can settle in to isolation and let our minds continually recycle, trying to wrap around the unthinkable. Living with a shriveled soul in hibernation is a choice we can make.

The powerful emotions of anger and bitterness can keep us clinging to the past. "What might have been" and "if only" are powerful magnets in the black hole of our loss. We'll talk about forgiveness and its ultimate necessity in the process of moving forward.

I trust by the time you turn the last page of this book, you will have had a few smiles. I hope those aren't just from laughing at my adventures and misadventures, but also from a different perspective on some events in your own life. My new life embraces love, laughter, and sometimes lunacy. May yours be just more love and laughter, without the lunacy part.

When I returned from my first project adventure, I treasured the opportunity to talk with Wess Stafford, head of Compassion, International. This visionary man has lived more adventure and gained more wisdom than I ever will. I told him of my misadventures and whined about how everything went wrong. He laughed! "Write it all down," he encouraged. "These will be some of the best adventures you'll ever have."

In my heart I thought, "You're kidding!" Three years later, I knew he was right. It's more than just a new beginning; I've arrived at a party I did not know I'd love.

My friend, I don't know the party ahead for you. But let's start the journey.

1
The Biggest Loser Is . . .

Lost: your dream, your cozy home, your career, the job you thought would carry you through. Lost: your marriage. Lost: the last breaths of life of someone you cherish—your child, your soul mate, your mom or dad.

Each loss is different. Though some are more sudden, others engulf our lives slowly, one foreclosure letter at a time, one cancer cell at a time, one inch of water at a time. Some losses thrash us in an instant: "Put your personal belongings in a box. An officer will accompany you to the door."

Crisis means we're punching numbers on the phone—911 numbers we never thought we'd punch with such desperation.

But here we are.

Of course, I don't know your story. But you have one, or you would not have picked up this book. I have my stories, but this book is not about me. It's about you, where you are now and where you *can* be.

There are "survival" books that just don't raise the future bar high enough for laughter, love, and adventure. These should not be considered possibilities for people after great losses, but actual probabilities. I want to try to paint that picture with words and a practical perspective that will turn your head from facing backward to looking ahead expectantly and then moving forward, from pain to gain, from loss to love and laughter.

Likely you feel beaten down. Not just your bank account if you're in bankruptcy. Not just moving into a space you never imagined you'd need to cram into again. Not just rehashing why you lost your job, rehashing the "what-ifs." When you face the death of someone you cherish, your soul weariness is unreal. Your emotional tank is empty, and your body lets you know it's feeling the hit as well.

You may feel you'll be down forever.

But, my friend, the human spirit, though feeling crushed at this moment, is neither docile nor capable of being submerged forever. While you may not feel it now, or even believe my words now, there is an irrepressible possibility within you for a different life you can't imagine at this moment.

Our human spirit is resilient beyond our imagination. But that strength, even rebirth, seldom exerts itself when life is smooth and easy. When income is steady, creativity is unnecessary. When good health and strength for the day are givens, seldom do we improve our diets and self-care. When death has not touched cherished lives around us, we seldom contemplate what is truly worth investing the last ounce of our strength for someone, or a cause that matters. A life of ease is seldom a catalyst to catapult us to a more meaningful, expansive life.

When life happens, tragedy happens, whether we participated in the cause or not, we have that sense of loss. Whether we reel and are swept from our feet, or we feel just a gentle unsettling breeze, at some point we ask ourselves, "Where do I go from here?"

It's not uncommon for our thinking to be clouded by thoughts of "I'm a loser." We remember with anguish folks people have branded as losers, and now we're doing that to ourselves. Let's change that script like a popular television show once did. At that time, they gathered folks who had poor health habits that had resulted in unhealthy bodies and too many pounds. The competition to slim down was a good thing and the biggest loser was actually the winner: a healthier body, money, and other perks as well.

We can change our big loser events into big winner outcomes.

You can live a life you never would have lived had this crisis not happened. But don't let me convince you; rather let the evidence roll.

Steve Jobs was once squeezed out from Apple, the company he birthed. Apple is now the most valuable company in the United States. Valued at $338 billion, it creates products that Grandma Hattie would never have dreamed of. She and Aunt Minnie would be shocked at the things I can't live without today that did not exist in their world, like Apple computers, iPads, and iPhones. Steve created this company, led it most of the way, and was key in its huge success.

We don't know how long Apple will be the most valuable company, the hot stock to own. But Steve Jobs came back after being squeezed out to become the human symbol of technology, creativity, management, and marketing acumen. He had a career most would envy. And, remember, he was once, for all practical purposes, fired!

Having lost his battle with pancreatic cancer, Steve Jobs leaves a legacy of innovation, a company responsible for the employment of almost 60,000 people, the most admired company in the world since 2008. Customer loyalty for Apple products is unprecedented. Would Jobs have envisioned such success back in 1985 when the board removed him from management decisions and he resigned rather than stay on the sidelines? One can say that Jobs experienced quite a party in his life after that initial loss.

Basketball star Michael Jordan was cut from his high school basketball team his junior year. He is regarded as the greatest basketball player of all time with an average of 30.12 points per game, achieving ten championships with seven in a row.

Opera singer Marion Anderson was denied the opportunity to sing in Constitution Hall on Easter Sunday because of her color. This rejection marked a milestone in the Civil Rights movement. The president's wife at the time, Eleanor Roosevelt, arranged for her to sing on the steps of the Lincoln Monument instead. Overnight she became an icon. Dr. Martin Luther King was in the audience.

My friend Ginger found herself in an unimaginable nightmare. Ginger initially experienced all the negatives of being the biggest loser. When her husband was incarcerated, she lost her marriage, her job, her home, her insurance, and her identity. Here are Ginger's own words:

"Top 5" Things Lost in One Year

My Marriage. Our once secure, thriving marriage of sixteen years was changed forever due to a prison sentence my husband received for white-collar crime.

My Job. My successful, full-time job as the CFO of three businesses was lost.

My Insurance. Both medical and dental coverage for our family were gone as a consequence of losing my full-time position.

Our House. The town house where we lived for ten years was lost through foreclosure.

My Identity. I no longer knew who I really was as I struggled to redefine my roles and purpose in life as a wife, mother, management executive, and sole provider for six children ages three to sixteen.

The Ginger I know today, many months into this ordeal, has become a more direct, loving, Mama Bear mom. She's discovered financial resources and ways to live on less that few of us ever imagined. Working with flexibility in a part-time job, she juggles being personal taxi driver, homework supervisor, home manager, and single parent for her growing children.

Ginger's small space is so efficiently utilized, you'd think it was her home of choice. I see her identity changing to become self-sufficient in ways not only necessary, but satisfying. And more changes are yet to come. We'll come back to her story later. But for now, are you beginning to see, as I am, an indomitable spirit within that Ginger never knew she had?

As I've listened to people in their times of loss, I recognize that we share similar experiences. Life as we knew it stops. In our jumbled thinking, we first try to analyze and sort it all out, to make sense of the chaos. "What If?" is the major theme. In the process, we discover a new view of people and things. Unwanted change brings surprises in our perceptions. We also feel alone—and in fact we may be. This becomes a foundation for new connections. Let's explore these shared experiences.

WHAT IF?

What's the difference between the person who stays in the stagnant space of looking backward, whining, bitter, and even taking on the permanent mantle of "victim," and those who begin to see a glimmer of hope and grasp it with a tenacious grip they never knew they had?

The answer depends on what they do with the big "What If?" question.

First, let's be honest and admit that we all do play the what-if game.

If I had parented differently, my child would not be . . . addicted, incarcerated, involved with the wrong crowd, whatever. The list of what-ifs for parents of struggling children, even adult children in their fifties, is endless. This particular what-if is a double-barrel loss. First we revisit every mistake we ever felt we made while raising our child who is troubled, destroying his or her own life, or at least not moving forward by our definition of success. Second, we are tempted to compensate by overcare, overinvestment, overindulgence, and overcompensation. These overreactions deplete us, and keep that child—young, middle-aged, or vintage—in a dependent state.

If I hadn't taken out that home equity loan . . . I wouldn't be facing this foreclosure. The national foreclosure rate is now one out of every 583 homes in the United States. Realtors predict millions more in the next few years. The upside is for those who purchase that foreclosed home at a savings. Here is the percent saved in several states by purchasing that foreclosed home.

52% Maryland
47% Illinois
44% California
44% New Hampshire
44% Michigan
42% Delaware

42% Tennessee
40% Wisconsin
40% Ohio
40% Oklahoma[1]

However, that savings to so many buyers also represents great loss for many others. Those numbers represent people who have lost their homes, and you may be one of them. The buyer may have saved from 40–52 percent of your home's value. But the money they saved is money you lost. Losses are rarely lone events. That home loss likely represents loss of credit rating, loss of treasured memories, and devastation to your personal pride.

If only I had not charged all that stuff, I wouldn't be sitting in this bankruptcy office today. That assessment of blame may be perfectly correct, but planning a solution and forgiving yourself while committing to a different future is better than rehashing why you purchased each item you could not afford.

My friend Ginger moved from 1,900 square feet to 1,100 square feet with her family of seven. Other young widows, families, and adult children have had to move in with parents or friends. So an initial devastating loss is accompanied by loss of solitude and personal space. As difficult as this sounds, I've heard many follow-up stories, of three-generation regroupings who've made huge changes learning to flex with the needs of the new family group. They've come to love and appreciate each other in a way they never would have experienced had they not combined their households.

The three recent home foreclosures in my neighborhood all started with divorce. Personal esteem usually hits the skids among the many losses with divorce.

I've listened to close friends in painful divorce proceedings go through a lengthy list of what-ifs. Secret keeping, wandering affections, addictions, self-centeredness, overspending, excessive thrift, hoarding, giving away too much, being in denial, being truthful or blunt—the if-only lists alone could fill a book. While divorce, of course, means loss of your spouse, typically a squadron of other losses accompanies this:

Loss of companionship

Loss of support—financial, intellectual, social, and emotional

Loss of hopes, plans, and dreams

What-if thinking is normal, common. Thankfully there are support groups and you may even have trusted friends and family to come alongside you, and be a measure of reality against what your perceptions might be.

 Life happens! Crisis, chaos, brokenness, death, and destruction are part of every human's experience.

There is some value in spending some time and mental and emotional energy considering the what-ifs. We humanoids have the capability of *learning* from our mistakes. Let me share exhibit A from my own life.

I love hiking, especially hiking with women friends in new places. We've hiked Acadia National Park in Maine, and also headed to Oregon for new adventures. The trails were beyond awesome, beautiful, serene, and sometimes strenuous. One Oregon stop was Crater Lake, the deepest, purest lake in North America. We hiked its rim and marveled at the change of water color as light and sunshine touched its surface and depth with lavender, even magenta, and more shades of blue than I have ever seen.

A boat ride was available so we trooped on, settled in, and began to see this work of nature, the handiwork of our Creator God, up close. The ride was too short; I hungered to experience more of Crater Lake. As we landed and prepared to leave, an additional option presented itself. A few folks (in hindsight I realize they were mostly young people) were leaping into the lake from a cliff. Intriguing! Our family has, many times, jumped from the twenty-foot cliffs above Table Rock Lake, Missouri, into the warm, summer waters—a pleasure indeed. Two from our group, our fearless leader, Carol, and myself, trooped up the path to the jump point.

Hmmm. Thirty feet looks a lot higher than twenty feet. My mind was not computing that the water was sixty-six degrees—in other words, COLD. Also, that temperature means the molecules are more tightly packed together, more like a board than a soft comforter. These facts weren't getting my attention.

What I was very aware of, in every nerve of my body, was the beauty below that I must enter, experience, feel! I could imagine the sunshine in the free fall on my face. Wouldn't the sheer beauty of this water be heaven-like to enter?

I leaped.

The descent was more than I dreamed. Descending through the clean, pungently scented air was a once-in-a-lifetime experience. As I neared the water, its colors seemed rainbow-like in variety and softness, yet intensely exciting. Exquisitely alluring Crater Lake beckoned. And then I hit water.

Immediately I knew something was terribly wrong. In one instant, I wondered if my legs would move. Pain told me something was amiss. I seemed to be going deeper from any dive I'd ever taken. Then—yes, my legs moved. And even the pain could not take away the gift of the beauty of the multicolored layers of water that I plunged down through and then began to rise through; they were more exotic than I had imagined.

Eventually I surfaced, thankful for all my moving parts. The rocky place where one could clamber onto the shore looked much farther away than it had from my lofty dive point. There were no options, but simply a requirement to swim to it.

Can you imagine being thankful when your knees hit submerged boulders? I was glad to feel them. It meant I could climb out! Carol sat on a magnificently shaped protrusion looking like a mermaid. I was glad to reach her outstretched hand.

It would be weeks later, after lots of black and blue skin returned to normal colors, when I conceded that something else was wrong and went to my orthopedic doctor. The diagnosis? Compression fracture of vertebra lumbar one. Had the broken bone moved one more inch, my spinal cord would have been severed—and there would have been no walking, no swimming, no leaping again.

Why confess this goofy, impulsive, practically life-threatening act to you? Because I've learned from it. The first and obvious lesson: No more cliff jumping (especially with my Medicare card tucked safely in plastic in my hiking bag!).

 At some point we must simply stop the questioning.

Actually, I've learned several more valuable lessons from this. One is that my adventuresome spirit can morph into risk-taking. I need to pause and consider the possibilities. Is this risk worth taking? I also learned that my children are still adjusting to the loss of their dad. My foolish action frightened them. "What will Mom do next?" I needed to think more thoroughly about possible outcomes and about impact on others who care about me.

Life happens! Crisis, chaos, brokenness, death, and destruction are part of every human's experience. Some good can be derived from pondering "What If?" Evaluating our behavior keeps us from repeating our mistakes. What was our part? What might we have foreseen? Were we part of the catalyst? Could our actions and reactions have led to a different outcome?

Realize that you and I may never be able to figure out the answers to all these questions, though. If other people are involved, we do not control them. In fact, we often discover that we have less influence than we thought. Weather, another driver, a law we ignored, medications, and reactions—the list of variables we can't control could go on forever.

The truth is, at some point we must simply stop the questioning. At some point we've got to take our what-if lists (whether they're written or simply rolling around in our minds getting bigger like a snowball rolling downhill), crumple it up, and throw it away.

What might help you do this? One friend wrote the long list and literally lit a match, put it to the paper, and watched it burn.

Another imagined the what-ifs as if they were taking up many rooms. She mentally gathered them up and pushed and squished them into a small compartment. She closed that door. When her mind wants to wander into that compartment, she sternly refuses to go there.

Most of us must realize that if we cannot truly let go and stop the what-if stuff, we must compartmentalize it, confining it to a limited piece of our thought life. If we don't, the endless cycle of unanswerable questions will impact today's behavior and tomorrow's plan. And that won't be pretty.

How sad it is to see an adult who behaves irrationally in some circumstances, or childishly, in irresponsible ways and says, "It was because . . ." They put forward an event or person as the "reason" (actually, an excuse) for their problem or ongoing weirdness.

"When we were teens, you . . ."

"In my first marriage . . ."

"I've never gotten over . . ."

"You made me . . ."

These people expect the world and folks around them to tolerate their inappropriate, rude, or bad behavior because they have not resolved their "Where do I go from here?" question.

I sometimes compare those insistent what-ifs to papers in an old-fashioned file cabinet. Nowadays we tend to file things electronically with unlimited space. But the old-fashioned file cabinets had only a few drawers and limited storage room.

In my comparison, we throw all the stuff of loss and all the hurt and brokenness that goes with it into the file cabinet of life. While some good can actually come from sorting through the "files," trying to make what sense we can out of seemingly senseless behavior and aftershock. And some good can come from throwing away certain questions, theories, and even memories. A bit of sorting is necessary or it's simply impossible to close the drawer with the overflowing mess. But closing that drawer with things in as much order as we can muster provides a great sense of peace and freedom to move on.

A word of caution: Sometimes a memory box, well filed, flies open at an inconvenient time. For example, I've wept at the silhouette of a stranger in an airport who so resembled my husband—and he's been gone five years. What did airport security and the other hurrying travelers think of this weeping solo woman? I cared little and could control my tears even less. That memory box had to be quickly shoved closed as I had to get through security collecting all my stuff and rush for a remote gate or miss my flight.

What if? Sort what you must, discard what you can, and compartmentalize the rest so the endless rehashing does not weigh down your future. We'll talk more about this in the next chapter. But let's look now at a likely positive outcome from your loss that you may not have noticed yet.

THROWAWAY PEOPLE

There's an amazingly helpful new discovery that can be made in the midst of loss. If you have not experienced it yet, I can promise you that you will. And you'll be richer in spirit for this discovery. I'll illustrate it through a story found in the Old Testament.

I trust you find, as I have, that we have a source of great strength and insight in the most-read book in this world, the Bible. I'm especially intrigued by David. His adventures, messes, and triumphs have him firmly in two camps: a humanoid who can get it all wrong and an admirable mentor who can show us how to live life boldly and well. Read leisurely through 1 Samuel 30, letting your imagination create mental pictures. Meanwhile I'll summarize this unusual event.

David and his army of men had followed the Philistines, ever their enemies, leaving their families and children in Ziklag. They returned to find that the Amalekites had raided the town, capturing all their wives and children and burning everything to the ground. Their first wave of emotion was grief. Grisly, strong, courageous warriors wept, and wept loudly. To say that things did not bode well for captured women and children in war is a known fact from all of history.

Anger followed. These usually loyal comrades decided the disaster was all David's fault. Had he not led them away from their families? They talked of stoning him. One single follower, Benaiah, had killed a lion in a pit on a snowy day. As a group these mighty men of valor had killed hundreds, even thousands of their enemies. David had cause to fear for his life. He responded with two wise moves: he looked for and found encouragement from God, and he sought advice from a wise spiritual leader.

In his desperate loneliness David entered an "Only God" moment. He reached that moment when nothing could or would work. It was God or nothing. He had no lifeline to reach toward, no best friend, Jonathan, to confide in, no wife to console him. Only God.

God gave him courage again, which David would need in large measure, to hear the words of the spiritual leader. He was to strike out on a hunt to find the raiders. He would need to advance in front of his warriors, leading them. Remember, they were threatening to kill him. He exposed his back to them. This action took courage indeed. David was a leader acting like a leader.

David's traveling army came upon a thrown-away person. A young slave, sick and weak, had been thrown away. His owner had detected something wrong, decided the slave could no longer be useful and healthy, and left him. Abandoning him with no food or water was a death sentence, even if he had been well.

David's men revived the thrown-away slave with what we know now was "right on" recovery food. David questioned him and discovered this slave had been with the Amalekites' raiding party. He knew of the Ziklag kidnapping and the location of the Amalekites' stronghold.

For David, noticing and then being kind and caring to this throwaway person was life-changing. The Amalekite slave owner's discard became a treasured resource.

What followed? A long battle, the total recovery of families, and gained flocks and herds. As is usual with humanoids, the ending was not all happy. People squabbled and were greedy. But we see here an important truth: Throwaway people exist, and their numbers increase with times of loss, chaos, and crisis.

The person who is perceived as weak, the one who doesn't seem to add to our worth or further our purposes any more, becomes a cast-off casualty.

Often we don't know these throwaway people exist, or we ignore their plight until we're in a hard place. But when we hit the hard places ourselves, something turns in our souls. It's called compassion. We see the invisible hurting child, the weeping mom on the two-year anniversary after her teenage son was shot, the barbed wire and razor metal defining the edge of the prison while defining the reality of the hundreds of inmates crowded within. Suddenly we see the hurt because we are hurting. Suddenly the prison is more than a place we look away from. It's home to someone we love.

 Loss means less, but less is not always a bad thing.

We see the teen athlete who always needs a ride home and has no one to cheer him at competitions. When the referee raises his victorious wrestling arm in victory, his searching eyes scan the stands. But those whose approval he most seeks are not there. The known presence of a parent who is there for him is a comfort he'll never have.

Our own suffering opens our eyes. We see the previously unseen. Their pain touches us. We connect. Sometimes the connection comes because we've become that throwaway person ourselves, or at least we feel like it. We recognize a truth that our Creator has known from the time He formed the first human, through the conception of each and every person who has ever breathed on this planet: There is value and purpose for us all.

We come to the realization that there should be no throwaway people.

So whose lives were changed by the discovery of the dying slave along the path of David's soldiers? This young man, who is nameless in the story, had a future. I'm sure David kept his word and protected him. Since this slave's scouting direction meant the entire army received back their wives and children, I would expect that all of David's army and their families included him in their community. Did he return to Egypt, reunite with his relatives, have a family of his own? We don't know.

Did David ever ignore a sick, young, abandoned slave after this encounter? I imagine not. I would expect that David, a man "after God's own heart," felt compassion and saw value in people who had been invisible to him before.

Andy Andrews, the author of *The Butterfly Effect*, was homeless in his teen years. His fellow homeless friend actually became his valued mentor, teaching him important lessons in life. As they walked around a hotel swimming pool, where a kind employee allowed them to "bathe," using towels to dry, his friend unexpectedly pushed him in the deep end of the pool. Shocked and surprised, Andy asked, "Why?"

"Welcome to life," his fellow homeless friend answered. And the friend began to talk about how you recover, how you treat those who mistreat you, how you move on. These days of Andy's literary success have not crowded out nor diminished Andy's respect and the treasured lessons he learned from his fellow homeless mentor.[2] I'm sure the homeless we do not see are in plain view to Andy.

After your loss, you'll notice people you never saw before. They are all around you. Look around more closely. You'll see others that were invisible to you before—others shopping in the resale shop, others at the food pantry. We develop a new appreciation of Jesus' prayer He taught us: "Give us this day our daily bread." Daily bread is the only thing Jesus taught us to ask for. Most of us have that in abundance, but many invisible people do not.

You'll hear of folks who've shared a similar experience to yours. You may even reach out. You may be in similar groups for courage yourself, and you may even encourage and strengthen others when you've been on the journey long enough.

Your sense of isolation and despair will be forced back by the knowledge that you are not alone. Of course, no one's loss is just like yours. But there are common threads, and you are strengthened and comforted by "like" shed tears.

THROWAWAY THINGS

People are more important than things. Right!

It's just stuff. Right!

You can't take it with you. Right again!

If the things around us, left in the aftermath of loss, are just stuff, why do they become so important in our struggle to move forward? Because our emotions ramp up and heighten their value. Factual value has been swamped by feelings.

Loss wraps its fingers around our budget, stomach, our heart, and the warmth of our bodies in winter and coolness in summer. We're different from the people we were before our loss. We whine and complain about loss of income, financial equity, and comforts we had when we had more.

Loss means less, but less is not always a bad thing. Less stuff means less to worry about, keep up, protect, and manage. Having less can mean time to do something else that's not stuff-focused.

But that's easier said than felt and done. The fact is that inanimate objects sometimes take on a life of their own due to loss. How important is this reality? A popular television show, *Hoarders*, illustrated this in its extreme. A real person, in a real living space, collects and collects until normal living is crowded out of his or her life. Some shop randomly in stores and at garage sales. They can never part with an object though it may be useless, or they have four hundred shirts, most of which will never be worn. The camera crew must crawl through tiny paths that are a maze through crammed spaces. Usually spouses and children abandon the hoarder if they possibly can.

Hoarders are an extreme, but I use the comparison to make a point. Things have meaning. Sometimes in the wake of loss these things can have purpose and value, either practical or emotional. Other times they can become dead weights hanging around our necks that interfere with healthy forward thinking.

Since the things around each of us are as different as our losses, we'll start with simple questions that apply to us all regardless of that thing we are clinging to.

Question # 1: To whom does this belong?

Wouldn't you think this question unnecessary? Not from stories I've heard in my world. It's such a simple criteria and one that's overlooked, to everyone's detriment.

One young widow was devastated when the brothers of her husband took all of his clothes, tools, and other personal belongings and divided them amongst themselves while she was at the funeral home finalizing plans. The blow of the industrial accident that took his life, leaving her with two young children, was intensified by coming home to the second loss exemplified by his empty closet. She courageously required the return of her husband's belongings with the statement that she'd consider their desires for his things—later.

In the immediate aftermath of divorce, sometimes pictures are discarded—pictures that, if saved and tucked away, might be precious to someone later on. This is certainly a tricky call, and no one can decide about the value of photographs but you. If you can wait a bit to make that decision, time may bring perspective or even more healing than you imagined. Yes, it's your picture, but it might have more positive value to someone else later than it has for you today.

This question of ownership gets sticky in divorce, second marriages, and other messes in life. If separating parties can step back and let their consciences speak rather than their anger or greed, things are more likely to land with the person to whom they belong.

Question # 2: What is the optimal time to decide for you, given your circumstance?

Parents whose eight-year-old died suddenly were cruelly told that because they did not empty her bedroom quickly they weren't entrusting their loss to God. Widows are often the recipients of such unwelcome advice on dealing with their husbands' belongings. The reality is that some clean out that closet in the earliest weeks after the loss, while others wait months or years. What we do with stuff and when we take that action isn't about the calendar or other people's opinions or expectations. It's whether our actions are best for us and contribute to helping us move forward.

Children who lose a sibling or parent are often comforted to be given something personal to remember the person they loved who was such an important part of their life. A thing as simple as a comb or brush can be comforting and may even become a life treasure, not for the value of that inanimate object, but for the person it represents.

A worn fishing pole, a bit of wood trim from a burned home, a worn pair of paint pants with splotches of a gazillion colors—sometimes the unexpected can be a treasure worth keeping.

It's not uncommon for quilts to be made from squares from favorite clothing of a treasured person lost.

One tailor/seamstress provides a comforting service accepting clothing and fashioning dolls to commemorate a person lost. My young widow friend has had a doll representing her husband fashioned for each of her young children using his favorite clothes and reflecting his profession and hobbies. Fireman dolls, police officers, golfers, and moms holding baby dolls have become treasured keepsakes. This might sound extreme for some. For others, it's just the right thing in a season of life, a gift that in some season is a thing that matters. That doll may be hugged on until worn, but just for one season and then packed away. Timing questions have a way of resolving themselves.

Some good advice after any traumatic event is, Don't make any big decisions in the first two years after loss, whether due to divorce or death. While that two-year plan may be optimal, the reality is that many don't have that luxury. Divorce may require a quick home sale. Death of a spouse may mean the survivor can't make that mortgage payment. My friend Ginger had to lighten up her children's possessions of toys, clothes, her own belongings for kitchen, furnishings, and even keepsakes as she moved to their tiny townhome.

Question # 3: What is the true emotional quotient of that thing?

Professionals who come into the hoarders' lives help them see the real reason behind their hoarding. When they are being challenged to give it up to the Dumpster or retail shop, they hold on to that thing even tighter. An unseen void, maybe even unidentified before, is ruling rather than reason.

We don't have a professional peering over our shoulders coaching and advising us as we touch that object we're clinging to so tightly. So how can we evaluate more honestly the emotional quotient of an object?

One valuable measure is what I call "the tear factor: how much, how often, and why."

One thing that we have in abundance after loss is tears. These droplets of water that leak from our eyes at strange times, or that gush like a torrent, are one of the most common experiences we all share regardless of our loss.

I've watched a young man cry angry tears over being fired from his job. I've reached to hand more tissues to my pastor friend who had lost his wife. Just mentioning the kind of pie she enjoyed turned on that uncontrollable faucet, even though we were in a busy restaurant.

I've puzzled over an Old Testament Scripture that declares that God collects our tears in a bottle:

> You number my wanderings;
> Put my tears into Your bottle;
> Are they not in Your book? (Psalm 56:8 NKJV)

What's important about collecting tears? It's God's demonstration to us that He cares for us in our times of great sorrow. He refers to wiping the tears from our eyes. Between humans, that is often the most tender moment shared, one wiping the tears from the other's stressed, tired cheeks. From the thirty-five verses in the Bible that mention tears, it's apparent that He is quite interested in why we cry. God was not impressed by floods of tears from His people when they were whining because they did not get their way. They cried when they dictated to God what they wanted Him to give to them. They cried when they thought what they gave to God was what He wanted. And they were wrong. He wanted their tender, repentant, obedient hearts more than dead bleeding animals.

What's in my bottle of tears? Bitter, selfish tears? Tears over stuff I lost? Tears that I invested in stuff rather than in people? Tears of remorse for the things I've done wrong? Tears of sorrow for the good I could have done and didn't—because I was distracted by lesser things? Or tears of regret over time spent taking care of things instead of treasuring precious people in my life?

What's in your bottle of tears? Crying can be cleansing, stress relieving, and a positive change point. A time of weeping can become a time of separating the "what was" from "what is" and from "what I want" in the future.

I have a wish for future tears in my bottle. I want them to be tears of joy and thanksgiving. I have a wish for future tears in your bottle. May they be joy and thanksgiving over the new things and new people that fill the void in your life after loss.

Look again at that object you are clinging to. What is its tear factor? Is it that important?

Remember, loss means less, but that's not always a bad thing. Less stuff means less to worry about, keep up, protect, and manage. It means time to do something else that's not stuff-focused.

One reason we need to let go of things is that usually there are at least a few good new additions after our season of loss. To separate the "not-good adds" from the "good adds," we can ask ourselves this next question.

Question # 4: Does this thing represent my new life in a good way?

A simple example from my life is a very strange little table in my living room. It is a rescued table that my creative sister salvaged and painted with brilliant animal faces and birds, rendering its crooked legs in the likeness of the patterns of a giraffe. It's a very old table, but a recent gift to me. It sits in a visible space once occupied by my husband's oversized easy chair. While I do still have that chair, it's now in a cozy corner of a bedroom.

Much to the dismay of my daughter and daughters-in-law and their tasteful design thoughts, this table just looks weird in my traditional living room that also houses a one-hundred-year-old, functioning pump organ. The colors on this table are crazy. My sister could not find a brilliant enough orange for the parrot feathers so she secured what road crews use to paint the iridescent orange line in the middle of highways. I love this table! It's symbolic. I go to Africa annually on my new mission. Energized, focused, and having fun, this Africa endeavor is a huge part of my single life. The bizarre rescued table represents that. This table is definitely a "good add."

While the oversized easy chair might seem to be the right scale for that space, it represented my life before my loss. This crazy little rescued table represents my life today.

Recognizing that some things must go, ask yourself this question:

Question # 5: Where is a good landing place for this thing?

Does it matter? Think *Titanic*. Think Heart of the Ocean diamond, a blue diamond fashioned after the famous Hope Diamond. While its reality is not confirmed, the tale of the young lovers and the symbolism of that jewelry represent mystery, memories, treasures gained, and treasures lost. *Titanic*'s heroine, Rose, saves it for decades only so that, in her last years, she might return to the site of the sinking of the *Titanic* and throw it overboard. Celine Dion singing, "My Heart Will Go On," while wearing the replica, has moved audiences and popularity charts by moving our hearts. Star-crossed love happens, if not in our own life, in the lives of someone we love.

Our treasured thing may not be worth $2.2 million like the Heart of the Ocean diamond, but if it moves our emotions, thought should be given to a good landing place.

If your housewares are too good to discard, you might consider giving them away. Universities have struggling students who need a few items for their tiny kitchens. Goodwill and Salvation Army Stores have been my shopping centers when setting up my young adult son in a different state. Donations are good. Think who could use this, who would appreciate the meaning of this? Don't think discard; think recycle. Give this item a new life and yourself permission for a fresh start for yourself.

As you begin to look at your stuff differently, you might be encouraged by the words of a wealthy businessman. *The Financial Times* recently interviewed Leif Lundblad, a Swedish entrepreneur. Successful businessmen often publicize their formulas for success. His advice: Beware of wealth. He says, "I have money, but it's not good to have too much because you become a bit, I wouldn't say lazy, but things become a little too easy."[3] Lundblad offers a bit of consolation for those undergoing the stiff discipline of having to get rid of some belongings: Lost resources may be motivators for action! That loss might prevent your life from getting too easy.

Leif's wise saying has its roots in Scripture. We've been saying that loss is not necessarily less. Proverbs 30:8 reminds us, *"Give me neither poverty nor riches, but give me only my daily bread."* Wealth can tempt us to believe in our own invincibility, self-sufficiency, and lack of reliance on God. Poverty can tempt us to steal or even gamble with what we have. Life happens to us all. Our loss can be the beginning of future gain. A good buffer against extreme living and overvaluing stuff is to read the book of Proverbs and simply live by the book.

FINDING NEW CONNECTIONS

When we're slogging through life's rainstorms or in a season of life with black clouds around our souls, we usually feel alone. And sometimes we keep that reality a secret and try to "soldier on" so no one will know the storm we're in.

That aloneness may make things worse. We deny ourselves the encouragement of others. We're vulnerable to poor decisions in our secret world of pain. And we don't take advantage of knowledge and understanding from those who've weathered the storm. While we'll look at this extensively in the third chapter, let's look at the aloneness factor now and how it impacts us.

An intriguing archetype in movies is the hermit who has become a recluse. Bizarre behavior, strange surroundings, suspicion, misreading others' intentions: all of this makes for intriguing story lines. In the movie *Up*, the widower even pushes away the good-hearted boy scout. In old westerns the recluse poked a rifle out the window at any human who approached. While these may be fascinating characters in movies, truth is stranger than fiction, and we see these characters all around us. In fact, we may already be those characters, or we may be on our way to becoming reclusive if we move from being alone to actually isolating ourselves.

Our loss may cause us to initiate spinning a cocoon that becomes our hiding place.

Yes, it requires humility to tell someone of the storm we're in, and that we don't see a way through it, let alone out. We hide the temptation we're struggling with, fearing judgment and shame. But humility signals to God that we're willing to learn, willing to change, willing to stop being self-sufficient. Self-sufficiency is probably an unreachable goal at the moment anyway. Humility softens our hardened exterior and heart, and communicates to another person that we're willing to listen.

Rarely is it possible to push back from the strong pull to hibernate without *huge* measures of forgiveness. In fact, this is so important that we'll spend a chapter on the major role this plays in moving forward.

Determine, my friend, to find some way not to become isolated in your loss. It is typical after a significant upheaval to lose friends, watch family members become scarce, and find it easy to feel like you are the only one in the storm.

My friend Ginger felt isolated and alone even with her six active children in full motion around her. Who could she really trust with the truths about her husband? "Will they shun me too, just when I need them most?" she wondered. The answer may be yes.

Your concern that the people around you might not want to help you, or might even reject you, may be valid. That's why being proactive to find new connections will likely be necessary. You have choices. There are support groups for loss recovery, for all kinds of losses. There are empowerment groups for health improvement and weight management. Group support for gambling and other addictions, financial discipline, and all kinds of issues may be meeting in your local library or community center. Your church or worship center probably has some resources. Mega churches may provide a support group where you can enter unnoticed for a while until you are ready to participate. It has been said that the loneliest place can be in the midst of joyful people lifting their hands and voices in praise—when your own heart is breaking. Hang on, and remember that this time of adjustment is only a season. You can become that joyful person again.

The Internet can be your friend, or it might be a foe. You can follow blogs that uplift and inform you, or you can use this tool to escape to the wrong places. Look for sources of help and encouragement. Websites can contain new suggestions or reinforce what you already know, but have felt hesitant to act on. Women from every continent visit my website for widows. Of course, connecting person-to-person in real time without the use of computers would be nice, but a website could be a port in the storm, better than feeling you are the only one going through your particular storm.

Books can become companions and lifelines during this time of recovery after devastating events. Reach out for the influences that feed your hope and help you feel connected to others who have suffered and begun again to thrive.

WHAT YOU HAVE GAINED

We started this chapter feeling like the biggest losers, fearful of what losses might follow the initial traumatic losses in our lives. But let's take a minute to look at what we have gained.

New eyes to see throwaway people.

New compassion for those who were neutral or unnoticed before.

Less stuff in our life to distract us.

The precious awareness that we are not alone.

Are you beginning to see that where you go from here is not defined by your loss? I hope so.

Great loss usually means looking backward, clinging tenaciously to threads of the past. While looking back is necessary for a bit, we must eventually release the dream we've lost—whether it's a home that's now rubble or lost due to foreclosure, or a treasured relationship that's over.

My widow friend Ferree Hardy describes her loss: "Life changed forever that day. Widowhood was nothing like I expected. The pain was so deep it was frightening; and then it went deeper still, to a place where tears watered tiny, shriveled up seeds of joy and strength. Did you know they grow best when buried in total darkness? When you can't see them, can't imagine."

Ferree describes what happens in nature that can happen in us as well. Those tiny shriveled seeds of joy and strength have gone underground. But tears of loss are rivulets of strength that furrow to the most unreachable parts of your heart. And something new starts to happen.

Another friend, Dorothy, describes it this way: "In the darkness of the night the stars come out. The brilliance of the sun does not compete. It takes the quiet darkness to see the stars come out." She should know. Dorothy welcomed back her young husband and lover from World War II—not as the healthy pilot who went to war whole, but as a paralyzed man she would need to care for. Amazingly, he did eventually walk again, but during those months of hospitals and no good news, the dark of her night seemed endless.

And then the stars came out.

At this moment they are hiding in the dark, but the stars *will* come out.

My friend, your tears of loss, as you let the dream go, are watering the seeds of a new dream. You just can't see it yet.

2

You Can't
Have It Back

The distance between our heads and our hearts is typically only eighteen inches. However, sometimes, after loss, we feel our head and our heart have parted ways and exist on completely separate planets. Our head is on Mars, our heart is on Venus, and somehow our body got left on Earth.

In my experience, I have felt that serious disconnect between head and heart when someone I loved deeply was incarcerated, when my life-long soul mate and spouse lost his battle with Lou Gehrig's disease, and when a person precious to me was addicted to possibly life-threatening stuff. And that's my short list. Though differing in impact on my life, each trauma sent my heart and head in different directions. My heart was clinging to, "This is not my real life. It's a nightmare from which I'll awaken to blue cloudless skies." My mind knew the truth. My body? Taking care of it was an afterthought at best.

What's the reality? There are probably not blue, cloudless skies ahead. But there are definitely new skies.

May I illustrate this head-heart thing with a ridiculous, funny, but true example? I live on a hill. Leaving my home to get out to the main road requires a left turn at the bottom of the hill. Making two rights when you leave my home lands you at a dead end.

My delightful, directionally challenged sister was in a stressful time of her life and marriage. Going separate ways and splitting their stuff, she ended up with a vintage 1959 Chrysler convertible that needed work. However, it was her only mode of transportation. Visiting me, she'd arrive with her three small children in the backseat. She sat, her tall regal self in the front seat, long red wavy hair streaming behind with a wide-brimmed hat perched on top, firmly tied under her chin, usually bedecked with flowers, ribbons, and a large feather or two.

On leaving my home, she'd go down the hill and make a right and then another right. Within a few minutes, she'd be passing our home again, making her way back to the main road. Reminding her to turn left had no impact. Bob and I actually began to wave our goodbyes and stay outside watching for her to make her two right turns and disappear from sight. Then shortly she'd appear again, beautiful hair and ribbons streaming in the wind, face resolute, driving toward the main road.

For some reason, her heart always wanted to turn right, and so she did. Eventually her head got involved in the decision, and she started turning left to make it to her destination. Time and intentionality were required.

It has been said that when stressful things happen, we should spend 5 percent of our energy and focus considering whether we got a good or bad deal, what the real facts and their implications are, and 95 percent of our energy and focus deciding what to do about it. The longer we spend muddling over our "bad deal," the less time and energy we have to focus on what to do about it moving forward. Focusing on the bad deal keeps the head, heart, and body on different planets.

Why is it so hard for us to gather the pieces of our loss, make sense of them, and move into our new lives? Because we're human. Turning right at the bottom of the hill seems like the thing to do. We resist change. Change requires great resilience, energy, and new thinking. Our brain has a "normalcy bias." We think the future will be what we believe, often based on the past or wishful thinking. Our battered emotions are confused, weary, and don't want to start new patterns. And sometimes our bodies are worn out at best. We even ignore ordinary upkeep of our bodies, which contain our heads and our hearts.

One of the hardest truths we must face is that we can't have *IT* back. In our humanness, we look back to what we had, or at least we thought we had. The familiar, though usually not as great as we remember it, was at least familiar. *Familiar* is easier to embrace than *unknown*. So we want *IT* back.

The truth is that no moment can be relived. Time cannot go backward. The event or season cannot be recreated exactly as we wish. Pushing rewind on a relationship is simply impossible. An important truth in embracing this reality is acceptance. If there are to be elements of our past in our future, *IT* will be changed slightly or transformed entirely into something different and unrecognizable by the event we have just experienced. Acceptance is key in bringing our heart and mind together. So what must we accept?

ACCEPTANCE

Accept that we're not in control.

There is so little we control in our lives, yet we usually don't bump into that truth until loss hits. Before loss, positive control seemed just around the corner. Now we know that level of control is simply not an option.

If your recent loss was a relationship, you may have spent a long time wishing and hoping in your heart that you would "get through" to that person. It's so easy to hope that the one we love will come around to seeing things the way we do. The reality we resist is, *It's not happening.* Behavior never lies; action speaks. Step back and truly recognize the action.

Let's assume you are disappointed with someone you care about. That person's decisions are slow. There's simply no progress toward mutual understanding. Here's an analogy from nature that might be valuable.

Think for a bit about trees in the spring. My willows become a beautiful green/yellow just when the Bartlett pear bursts into a ball of white that dazzles the whole neighborhood. Yet, the walnut tree is still brown, drab, not looking like much.

But all three kinds of trees are on their correct schedule. Given their DNA (if trees have that), the weather, their soil, and history, they're awakening as they can in spring.

Sometimes that person who's not blooming when we wish is more different from us than we think. We usually don't know the full story of our friend's life, challenges, and burdens. The more assumptions we make, the more likely there will be clashes in that relationship. It's easier to accept that a willow tree and walnut tree can emerge on different schedules and with different looks than it is for humanoids to accept radical differences in each other.

Those differences may eventually define and change our connection. But we can't even consider that step until we accept that we do not control them or perhaps even understand them.

Reminder: God has been patient with us. All humans have at least some regrets, times when our actions were in slow motion and our intentions lacking. God uses those times to teach all of us, if we're willing, to accept that He's created each of us uniquely different from each other.

Let's look at another analogy from trees. Storms happen. In my yard, I've seen a storm come through and twist out healthy, beautiful big pieces of my favorite trees. That same storm left dead limbs on old trees that I wish the storm had taken out. But storms do their own thing, not ours. The storm is beyond my control.

Life's storms, upheavals between people and their circumstances, happen. Sometimes we see what we observed as the best destroyed and the not-so-worthy still standing.

As hard as it is to accept human differences in each other, it may be even harder to accept that tragedy happens to good people and that life's storms are often just not explainable or rational, no matter how hard we try to make sense of things. A sober teenager of great character and promise is hit and killed by a senseless teen driving under the influence. A loyal, devoted spouse is abandoned, and divorce happens. Another marriage in seeming continual disarray muddles on.

We can't make sense of it. That's why acceptance is so hard—and equally necessary. Facing forward is simply impossible without acceptance.

We must simply accept the reality: We're not in charge of everything.

Accept that regrets are real in each of our lives.

It has been said that there is no greater sorrow than regret. It has also been said that there is no sorrow that heaven cannot heal. Both statements are true. But we're not in heaven yet. Most losses are drenched in regrets, small or large.

I recently was told by a broadcaster that he regretted not getting to know my husband, Bob, better, though they interacted through a common organization in significant positions on a small leadership board. I felt sorry for him. But there are no "do overs."

Those of us who have stared death in the face have a distinct benefit after our precious person leaves this planet. Now we realize the value of the moment. The treasure of a shared look of intimacy, the richness of a conversation that cannot be replicated with another soul, no matter how similar they are to the one we lost—we know now how valuable these moments truly are.

Losing a child through death changes parents forever. They are thankful for every memory of tiny fingers grasping theirs, of pushing their child on a swing, of watching the mess of that first birthday cake. If the parents have other children, they find that their parenting often changes. That loss reshapes the family parenting priorities and, in fact, Mom's and Dad's hearts.

When loss is financial and large, budget priorities change. Many unemployed young adults are learning to cook! Restaurant dining is no longer on the menu. That housing downsizing event has us looking at our accumulated stuff, stuff that we no longer have room for, asking ourselves, why? Why did we acquire that in the first place? Why do I own three Crock-Pots (and only two lids)? Why do we have a treadmill that does nothing more than serve as a support for my golf clubs?

We referred earlier to the five to ninety-five ratio that a popular psychologist has suggested. Allow yourself that 5 percent effort for thinking, investing emotional energy, and attention to figuring out the situation: good, bad, ugly, how hard was the hit? Now spend nearly twenty times that much effort in focusing on what you're going to do about it.

 ## Don't believe everything you think!

Applying the five to ninety-five rule, we can spend minutes pondering what we regret. It's time then to take the next ninety-five minutes deciding where we'll go from here.

So how is this relevant to you today, my friend? What lessons can you learn from regrets? Here are a few from my storehouse of blunders and moments, even seasons, I wish I could relive:

Remember in relationships that most arguments are not worth the swapped spit. Are there critical words on your tongue? Hit the mute button. Will that eliminate all regrets? Probably not, but at least you'll have fewer.

Have you lost home, money, or job? *Treasure the simple.* Much of what we feel is vital for our survival did not exist thirty years ago, or even twenty.

All work is worthy. Even if no one is paying you, do something productive. Volunteered activity is better than inactivity. You'll have less time and energy to spend on muddling over regrets.

Who are the covenant people in your life? Certainly your spouse and your children, and perhaps there are others. You'll have fewer regrets later if you *prioritize those important relationships* and try to get those right above all else in your life.

Let's look at another important roadblock that keeps us from moving forward after a loss: denial.

REALITY: DENYING DENIAL

Why is denial such snarly stuff and so hard to get past? Because it's so easy to deny that we're in denial.

Normalcy Bias

I mentioned earlier that our brains function with a normalcy bias. Let's look at that in more depth. This often explains why, when we experience loss, we stay in the mess, create a bigger one, or even move backward into a worse place than we are initially.

Our brains' normalcy bias means we think the future will be what we believe, often based on the past. Don't believe everything you think! History is full of normalcy bias that led to tragedy.

In 1935 Hitler's plans were emerging, and he was acting on those plans. One hundred thousand Jews left one city; 450,000 stayed behind, thinking that surely things couldn't be as bad as they seemed. When Hurricane Katrina was powering toward New Orleans, people were told that the levees would fail. Many didn't believe the warning and stayed. Scientists predicted that Mt. Saint Helen's would blow her top and spew molten lava over thousands of miles. Some folks didn't believe it and died. The human mind refuses to take in new information because we've never seen anything like it in our lifetime.

We like what seems normal to us. We don't know what change will bring. So we believe what we already think. Romans 12:2 addresses this issue right on: Don't be conformed. Let your mindset be Christlike (paraphrased). The majority around us may be 100 percent wrong. To be transformed we must become critical thinkers, look starkly at the reality we're in, and be willing to change. That's transformation.

The truth is we needn't succumb to normalcy bias. We can be straight-thinking observers, quick learners, and successful navigators of our new reality.

LESSONS FROM ELEPHANTS

Recently while watching elephants in Kenya and South Africa, I delighted in seeing them roam free. Seeing them in herds, babies bumping Mama's legs, munching—these were sights I had never expected to see in my lifetime. When we think of elephants, we think of wrinkly, baggy skin—and that image is true—and of elephants being very large—and that's also very true!

> Rarely can you move forward and accomplish the good things ahead alone.

But we don't usually think of elephants as quick learners and wise creatures. Those characteristics might bring dolphins and owls more readily to mind. But recently elephants have been tested in some complex situations to determine how quickly they learned. Food rewards were placed on a platform on the ground connected to a rope. The elephants were behind a fence. Two elephants had to drag the two ends of the rope at the same time in order to drag the platform under the fence, where they would be able to eat the food. The elephants learned to work together. One learned to wait before pulling until the other was in place and ready to pull. Variations proved that the elephants quickly learned the new challenge. If one was late, the other waited before pulling his side. Efficiently, they learned to get their platform of food for the benefit of both.

It's a simple example—bearing some profound truths! If elephants can learn to work together, certainly humans can try. It may be that partnerships and companions in your life will change. But rarely can you move forward and accomplish the good things ahead alone.

There are tasks you can't do alone. There are relationship changes you can't create alone. Wait, or possibly (we don't like this) move on.

Married couples, take notice. You can learn to pull together. You can relearn when faced with a new challenge. New babies and shifting budgets mean that the patterns of your past are no longer adequate. Challenges will come. Learn quickly, and learn together.

WHEN THE CHALLENGE
SEEMS IMPOSSIBLE

Do your circumstances today just not make sense? It's easier to stay in denial when you simply can't make sense of where and who you are today. Your goals and what you want to accomplish simply aren't matching the mundane restrictions of your real life. The apostle Paul had the same problem. In Ephesians 6:20 he describes himself as an "ambassador in chains." But wait a minute. Ambassadors are supposed to be people who travel. They "represent" in different locations. And they usually live in lovely places. Ambassador residences I've seen around the world are beautiful, protected, usually elegant and divine.

Paul was in chains—going nowhere. He was likely in a dungeon, or if on house arrest, not in the most comfortable of places. How could he call himself an "ambassador in chains"?

But Paul was effective in those exact circumstances. He wrote 24 percent of the New Testament while imprisoned. His epistles have been read by billions of people throughout the subsequent centuries. Somehow the brusque, outspoken, lawyer-like communicator just seems out of place in prison.

Surely Paul's heart's desire was to be in the thick of things, in the synagogues, in the public squares teaching and debating, in the homes of fellow tent makers, even on rough seas breathing salty air. Surely knowing the importance of his mission Paul was convinced that he'd get to his destination. But he didn't.

If God could make Paul's effectiveness increase in seemingly undesirable circumstances, He can do the same with you.

Take heart, my friend. Do what you can where you are.

THE TRUTH CAN SET YOU FREE

I met her in Burkina Faso: a beautiful young widow with three little boys to raise. Her husband asked his doctor to write two death certificates. He wanted one for his wife that stated he died of cancer, and one that stated the truth: that he died of AIDS. Facts are stubborn things, as John Adams once said. The truth is not always comforting. This widow had a right to the facts as she faced forward. Something within insisted that she learn the truth. Courageously she did her research.

I listened as she, with quiet poise, explained the plight of young widows like herself, and I heard courage unlike any I have seen and certainly wished I had more of myself. At that time I was seven months into my life as a newly single person. And I didn't like it. However, my four children were young adults, not dependent on me, and I was healthy. I wanted to be like her.

This beautiful young widow exuded a spirit of peace, even while not knowing whether her husband had transmitted AIDS to her. She did know that she had three energetic little boys who needed to be fed. She had no trade skills, and a small network of friends remained. Yet her spirit of peace spoke resolve.

I met this widow again two years later. I recognized her before anyone reintroduced us. Her smile of tranquility was her unmistakable trademark. I thank God she is healthy, and she has a job at a mission school. She started as a cook and now is a classroom assistant. Her teenage sons attend that school. God has smiled on her, and she shows it. But she had that sense of peace long before her circumstances changed for the positive. Knowing the truth and the possibilities, she trusted her out-of-her-control future to the only One who could help her through. She placed every breath she would take and those of her energetic young sons in God's care.

This widow could have been bitter and angry over her husband's efforts to cover his own wrongdoing. It's human to try to cover our sins, errors, and mistakes. If we cover them up, we need never ask for forgiveness or make restitution. But that's not God's way. This beautiful young widow chose the higher path for her journey. I'm humbled to have known her.

Are you gaining courage to shift your heart from the habit like my sister's two right turns to a dead end? Are you discovering you can reject normalcy bias and make real choices? I hope this story of my courageous young friend empowers you.

Before we move on to taking action, let's touch on another difficult choice. How do we know when we should walk away from a situation or person at a time when we're either in, or just through, a crisis?

Because I have no way of knowing your circumstances, I can't and won't give you *stay* or *go* advice. But I'll pass along some thoughts. Most of these I've gleaned from watching wise people, reading the book of Proverbs (which is incredibly instructive), and hindsight from my career as a counselor and life as a "vintage" person. I'm no wiser or more intelligent than any other humanoid on earth. But I have packed in a lot of observational living in my few short years (smile), tested lots of unwise choices personally, and would like you to be the richer for it.

WHEN TO WISE UP, WHEN TO WALK AWAY

Staying power is a good thing, whether it's in marriage through the rocky times or in parenting when your child's behavior is making you crazy. Marriage and parenting are covenant relationships before God, not business contracts. God allows for severing either relationship, but not for superficial reasons, and not without a process for trying to stay connected.

But staying put is not the wisest thing in all situations. Consider Joseph when his boss's wife was tempting him to sin. He ran! In fact, he took off so fast that he left his cloak behind. Read the story in Genesis 39. Temptations to marital infidelity are not new. There's a time when one must wise up and walk away. Walking away is always a tough decision. And often our closest friends and advisors disagree in their advice. Spiritual mentors should be helpful, but, remember, they are still human, as are pastors and church leaders. We often expect more than these humans can deliver. Remember, Job's friends disagreed and were wrong. And it's fair to assume that he was a careful selector of friends.

A temptation someone else can stand against might be our downfall. We cannot say that Joseph was weak in principle, moral strength, or conviction. Look at the hardships and abandonment he'd already experienced in his life! Still, he knew he needed to run.

One criterion is straightforward and clear: If we are required in our circumstance or relationship to violate God's Word, we're in the wrong place, or with the wrong person, or perhaps both. Wise up; walk away. Or run! This is much easier acknowledged than done. Leaving a job that puts bread on your table, leaving a spouse who is abusing you or your children—these actions often represent a leap into the unknown. As much as possible, lean into dependable people around you. If none exist, remember God is wherever you are. Remember from the last chapter, the "Only God" moment that David experienced? This might be that moment for you. He sees that your obedience to Him is so profound that you'll enter the unknown rather than not follow His direction.

Distancing ourselves from abusers is often misunderstood, especially when the abuse is a private matter. Remember we answer to God, not to other people. In families where children are involved, sometimes the truth is better unknown to others. Humans judge, and a child's scars should not be public knowledge. While we all would like to be understood and our actions approved by those around us, there are times we need to bear our own burdens. Like the individual soldier's backpack referred to in Galatians 6, not only is it our sole assignment, that backpack contains the supplies we need for the future. Galatians 6:5 states, "For each one should carry his own load." This seems to be a contrast to Galatians 6:2: "Carry each other's burdens, and in this way you will fulfill the law of Christ." There is really no contradiction. The burden referred to in verse two refers to those that can be shared with another as if yoked together to make the burden lighter.

Share when the yoke can be shared and others can help. But realize that some matters in life are private. The understanding and approval of others is not always an option.

DOING THE NEXT THING

Action. The moment comes when we must act—whether we're sensing a new purpose born from our loss or our circumstances are pushing us forward. If we're sensing a new purpose, we want something different and better to happen. If our circumstances are doing the pushing, we may be hanging on to the past like children clutching the beloved swimming pier, refusing to let go, kicking and screaming our frustration. But that summer season is over, and it's time to start the next school year.

Whatever is driving the need for action, we need to lean heavily into one of the greatest, most energizing and strengthening resources we have at our disposal. This resource is the greatest book ever, written by the One who Himself made you, whose intention it is for you to have a great future. Any wise, workable counsel we receive from any resource is usually based on the truths in The Book, though seldom does its Author get credit. Let's look at some of those facts.

You Are Chosen for the Challenge.

First swallow, breathe, and listen before you decide you don't like this truth. There's a saying: God fits the back for the burden. In other words, God knows you and equips you. Your backpack of troubles will not crush you. You will grow, become stronger, and make it through. First Corinthians 10:13 guarantees that "no temptation has overtaken you except what is common to mankind. And God is faithful; he will not let you be tempted beyond what you can bear. But when you are tempted, he will also provide a way out so that you can endure it." While we'll look more closely at the temptations in the next chapter and how we can overcome them, for now let's look at the match between our backs and our burdens.

We are challenged to have mustard-seed faith. Matthew 17:20 states, "Because you have so little faith. Truly I tell you, if you have faith as small as a mustard seed, you can say to this mountain, 'Move from here to there,' and it will move. Nothing will be impossible for you." Is Jesus literally saying that we can say to the Teton mountains "Move," and they'll move? No, He's pointing out that we can have faith for a tiny, ugly brown spot to grow into a large, worthwhile plant; this ugly brown spot in our life can be something quite fine, beyond what we are seeing at the moment. Our tiny, mustard-seed faith sends a clear message to our Creator that we trust Him to accomplish good things that are invisible to us at the moment.

Faith takes it even further to believe that you were *chosen* for the challenge. It requires a growing faith to believe that God allows a crushing burden *on purpose*. He is proving something to someone. We may never know what, who, or how. My husband was a superb example of this. When he entered the ALS support group with his confident smile and contentment despite his four-hundred-pound wheelchair and death sentence, everyone in the room took notice. He came to be a respected voice of comfort and strength, a man known for his faith. He was mustard-seed strong!

It's easy to be chosen for His blessings. Acknowledging that we are chosen for the challenge—that's hard. The two go together. God can be trusted for both.

Let's consider an important fact about our "backs" being adequate for our "burdens." God did in fact create you and me.

A recent international survey reports that only 28 percent of the almost 19,000 people polled in twenty-three countries believes God created humans, 41 percent believes in evolution, and 31 percent don't know what to believe.[4] I took my grandsons to the Creation Museum in Petersburg, Kentucky. The boys' foundation of biblical faith was strengthened as they listened, observed, and experienced the Godprints on us humans and on our planet. The boys themselves offered evidence of the marvelous variety and individuality of God's design. At that time they were all the same height, all within one year of age. But all similarities ended there. One sauntered, one swaggered, one floated—and we call that "walking." One grinned shyly, one beamed, and one charmed—and we call that "smiling." One sprinted, one sailed, one charged—and we call that "running." They were all walking, smiling, and running—but with such distinctive crafting by their Creator.

Biblical evidence is enough for me. But if you doubt God's individual care in creation, just watch people. Whether at a park, airport, mall, or athletic field, God's evident handiwork in creating people cannot be denied.

For more evidence, we'll explore the story of Benaiah. Don't you love a hero story? It's also a story depicting the old truth that things sometimes get worse before they get better. Benaiah killed a lion in a pit on a snowy day. Amazing! Benaiah means "built by Jehovah," so Benaiah was hardwired from conception to meet that challenge. We don't know if he fell in that pit that was dug to capture lions or if he jumped in to prove a point. Warriors sometimes do amazing feats. What we do know is that circumstances in the pit were not "normal." It was a snowy day—and that would be a rare event in Israel. One would prefer dry ground when contending with a lion. But it was a snowy day.

Can you relate? Have you ever been in an already-bad circumstance, and things got worse? Take heart, my friend. You and Benaiah have something in common. God knew your plight ahead of time. And, yes, you were *built* by Him.

This story from 2 Samuel 23 came to my mind recently when I was in Africa. I watched a lion kill a zebra on the Maasi Mara. How could Benaiah face such a formidable opponent? We know that "built by Jehovah" meant that God masterfully designed Benaiah's incredible strength and speed. God also knew on the days when baby Benaiah was crawling around that a future day would be his "lion in the pit on a snowy day" challenge.

Benaiah's father was Jehoiada, whose name means "God knows." How interesting! A generation before Benaiah was conceived, God knew and was forming the DNA for the next-generation warrior. He formed the family in which this young boy would develop.

Benaiah was from Kabzeel, which means "God has gathered." His amazing body was not enough. God gathered experiences that prepared Benaiah for that snowy day in the pit. Benaiah spent hours in preparation for days of battle. He spent weeks in battles and sieges, testing his mettle and courage. God was showing him His mighty right arm and its power at work in His soldier.

God had gathered every circumstance in Benaiah's life as a warrior to prepare him for that moment. That lion in the pit on the snowy day was no surprise to God. And the lion was no match for Benaiah. Someday in heaven, I'd like to ask Benaiah how he did it! But for today, I'll just trust His God for my challenges, which actually seem quite small by comparison.

Let's look at another truth about who we are.

You Are a Masterpiece.

You're a masterpiece! My friend Jo, a widower and parent of two teenagers, pondered Ephesians 2:10: "We are God's masterpiece. He has created us anew in Christ Jesus, so we can do the good things he planned for us long ago" (NLT). Jo was finding it not so easy to parent alone. How do you shop with your teenage daughter who loves trendy clothes when you are a career Marine? And what do you do when your athletic son still needs tender hugs from his mom, but she's in heaven? Jo probably did not feel that his back matched his burden. Yes, he could meet every criterion for the next promotion from physical, to mental, to tough decision master in the Marines. But how could he parent alone?

I quote Jo: "Problem is, a masterpiece seems to imply perfection, and I don't look back over the past three years and think *perfection*. While I have readily acknowledged the Father's hand in our lives and depended upon Him to sustain and guide my kids and me, when I think of my wife's death, my children's ongoing grief and struggle, life as a single parent, if I were a painting I'd say I am ripped in half and the colors were running together; if a sculpture then I am teetering on one leg. Perfection or masterpiece just never came to mind."

Look in the mirror. You're looking at a masterpiece. Ephesians 2:10 declares that we are God's masterpieces, whether we feel it or not. I like Jo's words: "A masterpiece created to do good things He planned long ago . . . the Father isn't just making do with me, despite all of my flaws. I'm the handiwork of a master, The Master, and He has good things planned for me. Reminded me of something I heard long ago; the value of a painting doesn't come from the perfection of the art, it comes from the hand of the master who paints it."

Jo could focus on his loss as a widower, his struggles as a single parent. Instead, he's focusing on the One who created the masterpiece Jo. I'm thankful for the encouragement of Jo's example. You can read more of his story on Widowconnection.com.

So, my friend, you are chosen for the challenge. You are a masterpiece. What are you going to do with that?

Just Start Something

Life after loss usually looks blank. We don't know where to turn or what to do. My friend, I encourage you to just start something. Start a new hobby, volunteer in a new place, reach out to people you've become distant from. Just start something. My attempts to teach young widows to sew in Africa brought challenges galore, surprises, and incredible comfort. You can try something new; the worst that can happen is that you fail.

And what do you really have to lose? Your new day may have seemed blank and meaningless anyway. Your new venture, laid bare before the Lord, gives Him the opportunity to step in and teach you. Just to have started something, regardless of the outcome of your efforts, counts as success.

When I first started with feeble attempts to teach young African widows the skill of sewing, I had no clue the challenges ahead or the rewards. I knew clearly that God left me on this planet on purpose. With my parenting days behind me, my career over, and my husband in heaven, I found it hard to believe that discovering a new purpose was possible. But then, these young African widows were more desperate than I, and I knew how to sew on a treadle machine. So I just started something.

We now have twenty-five widows who have graduated with skills in sewing that earned them not only their country's national certification as tailors, but also their own sewing machines. Now 179 children who lost their dads have moms who can make their school uniforms, sell garments, and walk with their shoulders erect.

It's not my doing, it's God's. Don't hesitate, my friend. Just start something.

Did I know that my seemingly valueless experience of learning to sew on Grandma Hattie's Singer treadle machine would one day be the basis for young widows to have a new life? Of course not. Did I know that becoming a widow would ignite a passion that catapults me out of my home, my continent, and my complacency into the unknown? Again, of course not.

It's OK, my friend not to know what the outcome will be. That's just not a reason to just stay stuck. There are good reasons to Just Start Something. Not knowing what's ahead does not justify inaction.

I Don't Know

I've returned from Africa, my seventh trip there. The continent never ceases to amaze me. While packing to go, I was quite aware that I didn't know what lay ahead. With every new country, there are views unlike any

I've seen before, food flavors like no others, unique smells, music, and clothing. I shared earlier the many surprises that on the surface looked like disasters from my first trip. While packing this time, I was reminded that this whole universe is simply God's footstool. What I'd see and experience would be no surprise to Him.

That reality meant peace in my soul as I packed for the unknown. I had never been to two new countries I'd be visiting. While the place would be unfamiliar, the person I trust would not be. I know Him. I didn't know what this adventure's surprises would be. But I knew He knows *me* and would equip me for whatever each day brought. Again, much of what I saw and experienced was beyond what I can describe in words. And the opportunities to impact lives are immense. And it's always good to arrive safely home again.

You and I both know that one of our biggest dangers is to become immobilized when crisis comes. When that tendril of hope starts to grow in our hearts, it can be quickly choked by the reality that we don't know where our new actions will lead us.

We have a better option than just staying stuck. I love the Scripture that says, "in all your ways acknowledge Him, and He shall direct your paths" (Proverbs 3:6 NKJV). God can only direct if we are willing to act. I remember one of my walks through the bush in Africa. The path was uneven; sharp turns gave no indication of what was around the next corner. The grass was taller than my head. Does your path seem like that today? You can choose to sit down. But then God can't direct your path. Remember, acknowledge Him in all you do, and He will direct your paths. Your boldness and action indicate your faith. He knows exactly where we are and what's ahead, and He loves to give us bold directions.

Let "I don't know" become your foundation for action based on faith, courage, and adventure. This may not be your ideal platform or one of secure comfort. But it's better than staying stuck.

"I don't know" often has a best buddy: "I don't care." The two work together beautifully to take away bright futures. You've probably felt this even if you have not admitted and labeled this frequent part of living through a crisis.

I Don't Care

Have you discovered that at the end of your most troublesome days, there seem to be two of you? One says, "I'm done. Giving up. I won't go to another interview. Subjecting myself to another stress-filled interview, followed by no phone call to report to work—I just can't do it anymore." Another you says, "But I tried. I learned something. Maybe it was not the right fit. Tomorrow will be a new day."

Losing a spouse, whether to divorce, permanent illness or disability, or even death can be the catalyst for the "I Don't Care" syndrome. My young friend Lisa, whose husband died at age thirty-nine of Lou Gehrig's disease, realized her own body had become the victim of the "I don't care" syndrome. I could *so* understand her experience, as our husbands' physical progressions and caregiving requirements were similar.

In times of crisis, we simply have no time for self-care. Caregivers understand this. Our hours and energy are consumed with doctor visits, insurance paperwork, tender feeding times, sponge baths, and tasks we never imagined we'd be doing. Our backs get weary. The clock says bedtime, but our to-do lists demand more minutes, maybe even hours. There's no time for that brisk walk, refreshing swim, or healthy salad. That five-hundred-calorie muffin and some tea are our midnight comfort. And that's not good.

Lisa faced down that syndrome during her days as a newly single mom after Andy's death. She committed herself to healthy workouts and healthy eating. Her "I care" attitude did not return because there was someone to compliment her. It rose from within.

Was it easy? No. Was it worth the effort? Her healthy body is now forty pounds lighter—definitely worth it.

Your "I don't care" moments might come from not getting encouraging or supportive responses from others for your efforts. Your efforts to move forward aren't being acknowledged or even noticed. So why bother?

Remember that Jesus feels with you. There were days when everyone rejected His message. He healed ten lepers and only *one* came back to thank Him. His brother James wrote that the double-minded person can't be blessed (James 1:7–8). He'd watched Jesus and seen His single-minded focus. Jesus acted from His inner motivation, not depending on public feedback or interest in making popular moves. Jesus is the ultimate example. Our forward momentum won't happen if we depend on feedback from others. We'll only become discouraged.

One reason folks can decide to stay in their "I don't care" space, is that actually feeling, letting the circumstance rock you, requires that you change. Your broken heart is fertile ground for new and costly actions. A broken heart is an open heart. Those bleeding wounds are a cleansing wash for something good.

Opening your heart is not for the faint of heart. If you doubt this, get to know a family with adopted children. Get to know a family who has adopted children from diverse cultures or races different from their own. You may never know why they took that bold action. But I can assure you that action was not birthed in complacency or an "I don't care" heart.

And the actions of these courageous families were not followed by, "They all lived happily ever after." You may not see their challenges, but I guarantee you they exist. There are times their hearts have broken. There are times when their love was not enough to fill the hole in their child's heart. The world's bias and unkindness was beyond what they could control. The damage of that precious child's beginning was beyond their fixing.

You can help. Don't ask them, "Is that your real child?" (I'm always tempted to answer, "No, it's my plastic one." Our humor gets a little crazy, of necessity.) Consider their challenges, their feelings. Often questions are based on the curiosity of the one asking, rather than in true interest in the family.

Read Scripture that tells us that heaven's population will be multi-colored and multicultural. Decide to create a little more heaven on earth by mixing up your own friendship network.

The blessings of an open heart, even an open heart created by brokenness, are huge.

Before we move on from the "I don't know" and "I don't care" syndromes, let me just offer one more thought. I call it the "But God" option.

But God . . .

When circumstances challenge us to reject their reality and woo us not to know or care, we have a better option. This is a prime moment for us to exercise our option of saying, "But God." We have a bigger, more powerful, more versatile, unimaginable, and immeasurable in its benefits, option.

You are richer than you think. You are stronger than you feel. How do I know? These two very powerful words in Scripture, *but God*, appear sixty times, each time this short phrase reminding us that things are not as they seem. Psalm 9:18 says, "God sees your need that is invisible to all others" (paraphrased). Psalm 73:26 says, "Our strength is small, but God is BIG" (paraphrased). Acts 7:9 says, "Joseph was sold as a slave, BUT GOD was with him and had other plans" (paraphrased).

Lay your problem out. Put your hopeless situation on the table and say, "But God, what do You see here? What is Your view? What should I be thinking? What are Your words of instruction?" Everything changes but God.

He has bigger plans, better solutions, and more resources.

My friend Margaret reminds us of the real question in those "But God" moments. The real question should not be "What was I thinking?" but "What should I be thinking? What perspective might He see here?"

I recently experienced a quick smack to my human reaction to a mistake someone made. *But God*, I whined, *the outcome could have been better!* (In other words, from my perspective!) I needed a quick smack. I was focused on what I wanted. God's very blunt and quick reminder to me was, "It's just your job to show up. The results of any of your efforts have nothing to do with you. That's My job." Scripture came to mind of the many times the tiny phrase "But God" appears. His line in the sand separates how we see things, what's coming down, and what's going wrong from the *But God* factor. Ephesians 2:4 NLT says, "But God is so rich in mercy," He loves us when we're unlovable, giving us positions and opportunities we don't deserve. Thank God for these *But God* moments.

"What lies behind us and what lies in front of us are but tiny matters as compared to what lies within us." Ralph Waldo Emerson's words accurately caught the importance of what really counts in our season of crisis, our time of unrest, our moment when life has changed.

The past cannot be recovered, rewound, or relived. The future is unknown. What we have is this moment.

Expending that 5 percent of our thinking and energy on what happened, good or bad, figuring it all out, is finished. It's time to put 95 percent of our thought power, reasoning, emotional energy, and even physical effort into what we will do next. What will be the next season of our life? Will we let someone else decide that we're a throwaway person or a masterpiece? Will we just stay stagnant, or will we just start something? Are we shriveled, or mustard-seed strong?

Given that loss always means there's a void in our lives, we know that voids are temporary. Something will fill that void. Push back sand with a tiny trickle of water, and more water will rush to fill the space. Suck the air out of a balloon, and it will collapse and there is no longer a void.

Given that our loss has created a void, let's look at some common temptations. I can guarantee from the culture we live in and the alternatives we face, that we have options. And many of them aren't good. They may sparkle, look appealing, and even be magnetizing. But they crush opportunity. Let's look at them and see how we can reject them.

Overcoming those temptations are the exercises that will create our just-start-something muscle. Overcoming will make us mustard-seed strong.

3

Temptations: Filling the Void

Empty is usually uncomfortable. Coming home to an empty house. Checking a bank account to find a zero balance or an overdraft, opening the cupboard to find only old crackers and a few cans of soup. A growling stomach. Less is not what we like. So we take action. That's not a bad thing. But a warning here is warranted. Filling that void is better not done on impulse. This is a good time to engage one's mind and talk with a treasured friend who has your back. You need to lean on the friends who consider your well-being their priority at this time in your life. You'll need to sort what matters to you. Often writing ideas down will bring clarifying, "Aha" moments. Keep your iPad or journal handy. Remember, seldom are quick fixes significantly good.

If a loss was unexpected and painful, it's likely that our first reactions will be extreme. We'll likely try to *overfill* that void, or we'll fill it with stuff that simply is not a match for the void. As I mentioned earlier, in the days and months I was caring for my lifelong lover as he battled terminal illness, often there was no time for me to eat. At the end of a seemingly endless, packed day I had a moment to grab something before collapsing for the night. If the 500-calorie muffin wasn't available, a bag of chips and a soda were handy. So often the quick choice is a poor choice. Loneliness because of a relationship lost is another danger zone for a quick bad fix.

There are a handful of very human tendencies for filling the void when we sense that empty space, that yawning place left vacated by our loss. While that emptiness is usually felt due to a relationship that is over or gone, the loss may be a thing—a lost home, a lost job, a lost investment, even lost status. All these losses trigger within us a bell that says, "Do something!" "This feeling is not like yesterday's feelings, and I don't like it." "Gotta get after something here so that emptiness will go away."

So what is that "something" that humanoids do when emptiness rolls in? Here are five popular actions we take. Note that I did not say appropriate, just popular.

We hoard. We accumulate, often at great expense to our wallet and reducing the comfort of our living space.

We hand out. We give, hoping that we might get something in return that will make us feel better. A better word might be *bribe*.

We hunger. We consume our favorite comfort foods or relational quick fixes. Those relational fixes are never really quick. There are always residual regrets or strings attached. Taking to satisfy is incomplete at best and destructive at worst. Only mutual give-and-take satisfies.

We hide. Rather than let others see us wounded, we withdraw. Hiding may also be an attempt to not subject ourselves to another loss. The risk of being wounded again is just too great.

We hibernate. Our hiding time becomes long, not temporary. We avoid the harsh climate of life by not participating in the human race.

If you're reading this book, one of these may strike a chord within you. Let's take a deeper look.

HOARDING

The popular reality television show that we mentioned in chapter one, *Hoarders*, fascinates us all. We watch, aghast, as the camera rolls over stuff piled so high that living spaces are no longer living spaces. They are dangerous pathways. Whether the stuff is valuable or junk, the reality is that the space is not livable. No dining happens in the dining room. Tables and chairs are covered. There's no family in the family room. It's occupied with more stuff. There might be a path to the refrigerator and probably a path to a space on a bed. There are probably paths to the necessary bathroom, but not necessarily.

Why are we fascinated? Because many of us feel a sympathetic twinge. We remember trying to crowd out a loss in our souls with some *thing*. We didn't take it far enough to be a *Hoarders'* television star. But we remember the feeling of trying to fill a void with something. We're especially vulnerable after a loss. The likely result is that emotion results in our spending on something that is simply not worth the investment, not even if it's thrift-store or garage-sale cheap. The investment will not satisfy our soul. It's money wasted.

So what's the difference between collecting things we enjoy, use, and love, and actual hoarding? Let's look at the definition.

Compulsive hoarding (or pathological hoarding or disposophobia) is the selfish acquisition of possessions (and failure to use or discard them) in excess of socially normative amounts, even if the items are worthless, hazardous, or unsanitary. Compulsive hoarding may impair mobility and interfere with basic activities, including cooking, cleaning, hygiene, sanitation, and sleeping.[5]

How is hoarding different from reasonable accumulation?

Hoarding is self-centered. Resources invested in excess cannot be used to invest in other good places or to help others. That acquisition is strictly for the hoarder. Typically hoarders hurt their relationships with others or are willing to do so—simply in order to have what they want around themselves. Regardless of the fallout to others or the price to be paid, the hoarder clings to that stuff.

Hoarding is excessive. A business executive might need several pairs of shoes given the career expectations regarding his appearance. Imelda Marcos, the wife of Philippine dictator Ferdinand Marcos, could rightly be identified as a hoarder of shoes. Three thousand pairs of shoes is simply excessive. Crossing the line from accumulation to hoarding may vary. But the next characteristic can define that line.

Hoarding impairs mobility and interferes with basic activity. On the

Hoarders show, one woman who owned a home was now sleeping in her car. There was no available space to lie down in her home. Now that's impaired mobility!

Another popular television show is *Pickers.* Two engaging men wander the back roads of America, bargaining for and buying anything and everything. Their "finds" are curious, intriguing, and valuable to somebody. They buy to resell. And where do they go "picking"? In spaces that look strikingly similar to the *Hoarders* spaces.

But there's a significant difference. The spaces where pickers find good stuff are typically in spaces that don't interfere with the mobility or basic activities of the owner of the stuff. Their living spaces are functional.

The concept of function, or purpose, brings us to a few reasonable questions we should ask ourselves when we decide to get something in a season of our life when we ache with the void of loss: *Will this purchase add value to our life circumstances at this time, or will it impair our ability to do the necessary things of life? How will this addition impact our future?*

 Our void makes us more vulnerable to accumulating stuff.

In 1986, a new phrase was added to our vocabularies: *retail therapy.* Retail therapy was first used in this sentence from the *Chicago Tribune* of Christmas Eve, 1986: "We've become a nation measuring out our lives in shopping bags and nursing our psychic ills through retail therapy." Now this common phrase has a definition and pops up in ordinary conversations. The definition: "Retail therapy is shopping with the primary purpose of improving the buyer's mood or disposition. Often seen in people during periods of depression or transition, it is normally a short-lived habit. Items purchased during periods of retail therapy are sometimes referred to as 'comfort buys.'"[6]

I think each of us, without much hesitation, can recite our "comfort buys." Like our favorite comfort food (mine is my own homemade soup), we know exactly where we migrate when we want to buy something that brings comfort. Whether it's a special coffee shop where the aroma soothes our soul, or Tiffany's where the dazzle crowds out the sadness in us, we feel better there than in our own space. However, being there has consequences and temptations.

The definition includes what should prevent retail therapy from becoming hoarding: It is a normally short-lived habit during depression or transition. The dangerous tipping point from therapy to hoarding is when we get stuck in depression and don't make a healthy transition.

Another danger signal is when the costs and bills are beyond what our budget can accommodate. Notice I did not say how high our credit card limit can rise. Card issuers are happy to let you spend beyond your means—as long as you pay those few dollars monthly that typically won't even cover the interest rate. Retail therapy has "comforted" folks right into bankruptcy, the divorce court, and relational disaster.

That special cup of coffee (yes, I've indulged in a cozy corner by the fireside warming my fingers with that cup to counteract the chill in my soul) did not impair my financial future. But a daily habit is $100.00 a month, or $1,200.00 in one year; and that level of spending might be significant. (Check my math. And then calculate any possible retail therapy habits in your life!)

I don't know what a stop in Tiffany's might cost, but if that's where you're headed, make sure you have extra cash in your pocket before you enter to soak in that dazzling comfort!

In 2001, the European Union conducted a study finding that 33 percent of shoppers surveyed had a "high level of addiction to rush or unnecessary consumption."[7] This was causing debt problems for many, with the problem being particularly bad in young Scottish people.

I noted retail therapy recently in a way I had never before observed. On two separate occasions in two different department stores, I observed customers making returns of several items. Being in line behind the customer, I found it hard to ignore the transaction going on only a few inches away, especially because I was in a hurry and the process was quite long.

The customer laid several return items on the counter and sorted through handfuls of receipts to find the matching one for each item. She returned those items, and they were credited to her outstanding bill. Done? Not quite.

Then the customer dug for an envelope and fished out a wad of cash and gave it to the clerk to be applied toward her department store bill. After that transaction, the customer clearly asked what the amount was still on the charge card. (I'm seriously trying not to listen and have turned away.) This scenario was repeated in two different stores, two different people, but the same routine: returns, partial payment, and still outstanding charges. In both cases the clerk clearly stated numbers more than three hundred dollars. In both cases the clerks were kind and patient. In one case the clerk greeted the customer by name, from which I concluded that the clerk would see that customer again soon.

Were these customers hoarders? I don't know. But their actions were not matching good budgeting sense. Obviously their shopping habits were consuming money they did not have and time that could have been spent elsewhere.

Stores do all they can to help you sense that feel-good emotion so you'll put something extra in your shopping cart. One technique for food shoppers is the careful way the store and products are laid out to shout "Fresh" to you. Yes, we are more likely to buy "Fresh."

At the front entrance are fresh flowers with the price marked on a blackboard with chalk. One thinks they just came from the gardener's truck. Color matters: That banana was carefully grown and picked at the right moment to achieve the color that folks like to buy. Those "fresh" apples were possibly picked fourteen months ago. And that mist action on the fresh vegetables? That actually contributes to their rotting faster, but the moisture makes you think the water and ice is keeping them crisper! So much for those fresh ideas that tempt us to buy!

It's certainly fair to say that stores will help you spend. That's why they exist. One tool we have during times of loss is "Don't step inside." Or enter with just enough cash for your necessities for that day.

We know these shopping temptations. Their appeal is not new. It's just that after loss our void makes us more vulnerable to accumulating stuff.

HANDING OUT

Another temptation, a relative of hoarding, is Handing Out. I've found no definition of this and have never heard of it related to filling a void. But I've seen it and been tempted by it myself. Many of you reading this book will understand. You may even identify that you've "handed out" to fill a void. I know I have. So here's my definition.

Handing Out: giving to another person something that costs you and is of value to you, in the hope that the person will stay in your life or invest something in your life, helping to fill your personal void.

For example, divorced parents, usually the ones without custody, might overindulge their child or children, hoping to keep their affections in this new season of life.

Similarly, a young widow or widower may overindulge children, hoping to compensate for the absent parent with things. The widow or widower of adult children indulges those adults with things or events, hoping to keep them even closer, filling some of the void left after losing their spouse. That empty space is large, and widowed people want more of their children rather than less. That expectation asks for disappointment.

Aging parents wishing for more relationship or attention from their children sometimes "hand out" things or cosign loans. That handout may extend further than children to other relatives for hoped-for friendships.

One widow with an empty bedroom allowed a homeless young man to move in. She allowed him access to credit cards, which he abused. Her children were dismayed but unsuccessful in getting Mom to send him on his way. He bought tools for his friends and clothes for himself. She paid a heavy price both emotionally and financially for bad companionship.

Making a relationship more desirable by giving things or providing experiences isn't making a relationship. Recognizing that without those handouts another person might move on, move out, or not move in closer is better done sooner rather than later.

News flash: Handing out does not work. The person on the receiving end may show up, short-term. But that person's being there for the wrong reason—accepting the handout rather than valuing the relationship—simply prolongs the important work we need to do. We need to focus on filling the void with what's good, what works for us, and what will be satisfying in the long run.

Handouts happen in organizations as well. A person in a position to hand out perks often does so because he's looking for people who will be loyal, agreeable, and available rather than someone capable for the "perk" position. Those passed by for the perk or promotion get the message: They're not in the inner circle, not valued. They may even get that pink slip and then watch their position go to a relative or social buddy while they head for the unemployment office. The void is still there, but there's value in recognizing the handout.

We don't need to take the rejection personally when we recognize that people with the ability to make the handout did it to satisfy their own needs, because their actions were not based on the merits of the individual.

HUNGER

Hunger is a normal appetite. Our body needs food for energetic activity. Our emotional tank needs touch for relational activity. But emptiness often changes need to greed.

If one piece of pie is satisfying, we think two pieces will bring real comfort.

My fishing friends had a great catch in their fishing basket. Ending a great day on Table Rock Lake, they were stunned to look at their fishing basket floating next to their boat. A huge black snake, contorted in shape from swallowing most of their fish, was trapped in their basket and could not get out. He had slithered in at one size, devoured their catch, and was now too big to escape.

How like the reality of our temptation for consuming something, our hunger to fill that void, resulting in gorging. If one piece of pie is satisfying, we think two pieces will bring real comfort.

Books, training programs, exercise series galore exist to help anyone change their consumption patterns. Weight Watchers, Jenny Craig, Alcoholics Anonymous, and workout regimens offer truly helpful tools for getting healthy. The question we must ask ourselves is "How long will the solution last?" That answer depends on whether we fill the void that caused us to consume with a healthy, satisfying solution. The pounds can reappear, or the substance abuse comfort become too good to resist, as long as the soul hunger is unsatisfied.

That void becomes a beast stalking within with an insatiable appetite. It becomes that snake trapped in the fishing basket, no longer free, but only satisfied for the moment.

How like the evil one, the great serpent of Scripture. He can slither into our lives, devour every good possibility of today and tomorrow. From all appearances, he won! But not really. We have better options. His day will come when the great Fisher of Men will claim us. And the great serpent will not be able to escape.

How often we attempt to satisfy our hunger with what worked in the past, even decades before. Menus in my childhood included corn bread with butter and honey, mashed potatoes drenched in gravy alongside fried chicken followed by apple dumplings covered with syrupy, warm caramel sauce. That menu worked for a teenager going out to do farm work for long hours. That menu for today? Disaster! That level of consumption is a mismatch for my lifestyle today.

If you have unsuccessfully battled destructive habits, been up one day and down the next, or successful for three months and then reverted to the old habit, consider this: Rather than focusing on what you must deny yourself, consider what healthy new action, pattern, or behavior to add to your life.

Usually change requires some added, new good thing replacing the old habit. Some of those might be regular meetings with support groups, memberships in gyms, or partnering with regular biking or walking buddies. You have options.

HIDING

An intriguing theme in many popular novels is the recluse. That curious person behind the curtain in the supposedly haunted house draws us. The grass is overgrown; the shutters are sagging. There are few signs of life except when a door creaks open so the recluse can make the rare excursion to the grocery store—or the cemetery. We are intrigued by these characters—because we've felt like becoming one of them ourselves at one time or another.

In novels, the big, dramatic climax usually comes when someone breaks through the isolation barrier of the recluse and discovers why that person went into hiding. Usually loss swallowed up ordinary living. A child died. A tragic accident took a lover's life. Their nest egg was embezzled. They were betrayed. And they went into hiding.

We close the novel and think, "What a waste!" How blind to the lost possibilities, the missed fun, the possible new relationships or salvaged old ones.

We are less likely to look in the mirror after our own loss, which, granted, may seem small in comparison, and see that we hide out after loss.

We've lost our job. We keep showing up in the same places pretending nothing has changed. We're not hiding out, but we're hiding from reality. The old phrase "keeping up with the Joneses" represents another form of hiding from reality. Our real choice is to change our lifestyle to match our real income. That may mean a picnic in the park rather than a day at a theme park.

We've lost our mate. Friends grant us some time to hide out. I felt numb and preferred to hide out. Invitations, while few, were declined, and I did not know how to behave in a crowd when I entered the room alone. I had no partner to signal when I needed rescuing from a conversation. I had no best friend in the room. Staying home alone felt better.

Hiding can be a good thing given a few conditions. Hiding should be temporary, and hiding needs to provide a space for healing. That recluse in the novel hides but does not heal. And hiding turns into long-term hibernation.

How do you know if your hiding is a place of healing? Here are a few questions to answer.

What are you thinking about? Are you continually looking backward, mulling the past?

Is the space around you deteriorating in care and appearance?

Are you taking care of your body in this "hiding" time?

Is this temporary hiding period potentially good?

Are you investing thinking time in the future? What are your options moving forward? The apostle Paul seems to echo that commitment to spending 95 percent of our focus on looking forward and only 5 percent looking back. He wrote, "Forgetting the past . . . I press on" (Philippians 3:13–14).

Are you regularly in contact with someone who has your best interests at heart? Even if a brief hiding time is healing, we risk losing perspective and becoming self-focused. Accountability to another person is even more important because we're hurting and vulnerable to wrong decisions and skewed thinking.

While we typically think of hiding as staying away from people, hiding might also be continuing our routine with the same people but hiding our loss from them. This is quite common when someone we love is incarcerated. Yes, you have the option of secrecy. But you may find, as I did, that letting some people, maybe even just selected people, know resulted in comfort and empathy in a time when I needed just that.

When I began to mention the incarceration of someone I loved in groups where I spoke and conferences, I found that a floodgate was opened. I can't tell you how many people would come to me in private and say, "I've never told anyone." And they'd pour out their hearts about their son, their husband, a niece they loved. Even visible, involved church folks were keeping the secret. Often I was the first person to whom they told their story. My advice? Find *someone* in your present network and tell that person. You need support and encouragement. Don't hide out!

HIBERNATION

Hibernation is a good thing for animals like polar bears and insects like caterpillars. But there's no evidence that it enhances the lives of people. In animals, hibernation is a state of inactivity and a lower metabolic rate. This is usually helpful in surviving harsh conditions like extremely cold temperatures.

Whether in caves, in snow mounds, or in the mud below the frost line, hibernating creatures are behaving in ways that are best for their future. They've fattened up ahead of time and know when to come out. Their hibernation is temporary and for good reason. They would die of starvation if they stayed outside that safe place. Their lower metabolic rate in their cave is necessary until outside conditions become less hostile.

As humans, we may see our outside living conditions as worse than they really are. And we may lose our navigational life skills because we're hibernating. We're unaware of current news and trends. Our polyester plaid jacket seems just fine to us.

The questions we ask ourselves about hiding out are good to ask again as hiding has extended to become hibernation. As we hibernate, the space we're living in often deteriorates. We lose touch with the reality of how the tattered space looks to someone else who has not been living in it.

One star interior designer discovered that he could help depressed persons move beyond their depression by improving the appearance of the space they lived in. Most of us won't experience that gifted designer swooping in with a few dollars and lots of creativity and energy to transform our space so it will lift our spirits.

But a great first step would be just to invite someone into our space. What happens? We begin to look around with different eyes. As I was writing this book I had to impose a temporary hibernation time to meet my deadline. Clutter collected—neglected mail on the dining room table, crackers and bags of chips on the kitchen counter, jewelry spread in abandon on the bedroom dresser, contact solutions and containers near the bathroom sink. And the phone rang! My friend is on the way to loan me an interesting book.

I looked around with new eyes and then raced about in overdrive, straightening things. And that was for a short-term, self-imposed, for-a-good-reason hibernation. But you can see the value of another set of eyes entering our space. Start by looking, listen to their perspective, and step out!

These five ways we're tempted to fill the void in our lives all successfully keep us facing backward—which is hardly success. The problem in facing backward is that we remain trapped in our loss and immobilized. We have a better option. Let's explore how to face forward.

STOP WASTING
YOUR VALUABLE RESOURCES

Henry Wadsworth Longfellow once wrote, "Great is the art of the beginning, but greater is the art of ending." His words touch on a point about the great difficulty of putting away what has gone before, with all its trauma, to make a new start.

It's not uncommon for that person who has freed herself from a bad place, courageously moved on to try to plan and experience a good future, to move back into the old mess. What happened? We look on with horror. One mom with two youngsters finally moved away from her abusive husband. Up and out finally! She was surrounded by a supporting cluster to help her get on her feet again. And things seemed to be going fine. Then she abandoned her children, placed them with caring relatives, left her new safe setting, and moved back in with her abuser!

What sense does that make? Why? How could she?

For a while, entering a new space—however positive it really is—can be more painful than the old situation was. We struggle with regrets, with indecision, with confusion. Thoughts chase each other in our minds:

That relationship failed. That means I'm a failure. Maybe I should give it one more try.
I can't believe it happened to me. I've got to fix it.
Empty hurts. At least I had something, and maybe that was not so bad.
I can't face that those ten years in that relationship were wasted years in my life. Moving on is giving up.

Before letting those thoughts mesmerize you, answer these questions with as much clarity and courage as you can:

What do you have to show for the last five years in that relationship,
or that job?
What do you have to show for the last ten years in that relationship,
or that job?
Were you loading on more debt?
Were you adding special memories and treasured moments to your
shared history, or simply adding fights and frozenness?
Were you adding healthy coping tools for making it through the hard
things and hard times?
Were you making healthy choices for your body?

Hard things and hard times happen to us all. We cope. But what tools did we choose? Have those tools been helpful or harmful? Are there any behavioral indicators that indicate that the next five years will be different from the last five?

Notice, I did not ask what promises your boss is making, or hints from that recruiter, or assurances from that special person that things will be different. In our culture the term "significant other" implies goodness and importance, a person of value in our lives. It may mean, in reality, a person unwilling to permanently commit, a person who does not value you enough to be your spouse.

BEHAVIOR INDICATORS

The phrase "behavior indicators" is a key one. When you're tempted to turn back, think in terms of concrete truths. What action has actually changed to make going back a good idea?

Perhaps those ten years or five years seem lost or wasted to you. Isn't it better to limit the loss and damage to those ten or five years rather than adding on another twenty?

Another description of opportunity lost or squandered is "misery repeated." Wishful thinking may simply be denial of the reality of the moment.

Resources are limited. You and I have been issued one body. We've also been given twenty-four hours every day—no more, no less. We don't know how many tomorrows we will have. Every day we spend reliving the past is a wasted resource for creating a successful tomorrow. Every action that is destructive to this one body we've been given is energy unavailable for moving forward. And moving forward takes lots of mental, emotional, and spiritual energy.

We've talked about voids in our lives caused by lost jobs, lost homes, and lost relationships. All of these losses hurt. But lost relationships are usually the most difficult from which to move forward, and temptations are greater to make bold, disastrous moves that make a bad situation worse. For that reason, let's take some extra time to consider the scenario of lost relationships. Perhaps we are never in a more vulnerable place to wrong thinking and destructive behavior than when we are reeling from a relationship loss.

One of the most important objectives to achieve in that time of void is making a clear decision about the person who is no longer in your life.

Who is/was that person really? When we answer that clearly and correctly, we are able to decide how to behave in the future. Even if that person is gone, he or she has power over your future. You may have adapted and have habits that were determined by that person who is gone. You may have changed your self-perception to match the perception that person had of you. You'll be reminded of the lost person in expected and unexpected circumstances. It may be when you open the mail or an email; it may be in visiting a setting familiar to one you shared. It may be the scent of familiar perfume or aftershave. At that moment, it will be easy to be that person you were in the past. But that reality is over.

Identifying that person accurately will determine whether that reminder will set you back, be a reality check, or give you pause to count your blessings.

How can you accurately identify who that person is/was really?

An expert on that topic is Henry Cloud. In his book *Necessary Endings*, he defines three kinds of people: wise people, foolish people, and evil people.[8] His descriptions can help in many life scenarios. Understanding the three kinds of people can help individuals determine when it's time to move on, or move away from difficult circumstances and people. But we're assuming here that your relationship is already broken; the loss has taken place. In order for you to move on, though, you must define that lost spouse, child, or friend accurately. Even if that person is both gone and dead, you must define him or her for your own healthy tomorrow.

Another expert on identifying people is Jan Silvious. Her basis for identifying people is their description in Proverbs. Henry Cloud and Jan Silvious agree on who wise people and foolish people are. Both accurately describe their behavior. With permission from Jan Silvious, I created a chart on the difference between wise people and foolish people in my book for widows, *From One Widow to Another* on page 118. For now let's look at wise people as defined in Proverbs. Cloud's descriptions are consistent, excellent, and couched in business terminology.

Wise people: Proverbs	Foolish people: Proverbs
Wise people listen.	Foolish people will not listen.
Wise people think.	Foolish people will not think.
Wise people learn.	Foolish people will not learn.
Wise people attempt reconciliation.	Foolish people will not be reconciled.
Wise people realize they are imperfect.	Foolish people are always right.
Wise people learn from their failures.	Foolish people repeat faulty behavior.
Wise people trust God.	Foolish people trust themselves.
Wise people think straight.	Foolish people don't think straight.
Wise people accept the truth.	Foolish people change the truth so they will not have to change.
Wise people accept responsibility.	Foolish people reject responsibility and blame others.[9]

Cloud makes the contrast that wise people respond to truth and adjust to the facts. Foolish people adjust the truth so that they don't have to adjust *to* the truth.

If you've read these lists and still cannot determine if this person with whom you were in a relationship before was wise or foolish, make two lists. What *behavior*, specific actions, did you observe that you can write under a "Wise" list? What *behavior* did you observe that you can write under a "Foolish" list? Let those actions speak.

I've seen a lot of behaviors that would fit well under "Foolish" in a list, and likely you have, too. Some people are still rationalizing their adult behavior on aspects of their less-than-desirable childhoods. "Mom didn't want me," they say. Or, "Dad didn't like me."

Another person blames his siblings for ignoring him so that he got in with a bad crowd. He still brings it up with his siblings, wanting them to take responsibility for his sorry adult life.

People often look for circumstances to blame: "I never had enough money to create a budget." Or, "I've seen so many terrible things in my lifetime, that's why I . . ."

Other folks turn the blame onto you: "You introduced me to . . . This mess is *your* fault."

It's also foolish to drag events and issues from long ago into today's argument: "Remember when you . . ."

Are you getting the picture? Negative, negative, negative. Poor me. I'm the victim and can't help myself. I don't want to be lonely in this cesspool, so I'll bring you in to keep me company.

Cloud says, "Just stop talking."
Silvious says, "Stop swapping spit," meaning arguing.

Conclusion: be grateful for the new void. The likelihood of a better future with a fool is zero.

Let's look at the third group that Cloud identifies: evil people.

Most of us were brought up to "make nice," tolerantly accepting the notions of "to each his own" and "different strokes for different folks." Few of us were trained to recognize evil people.

And then life happens. We discover there is evil on the planet in people—real people in our circles. That person with whom you had a relationship might be an evil person. Let's distinguish *evil* from *foolish*. The fool hurts you unintentionally. When a person thrashes around like the proverbial bull in a china shop, stuff and people get damaged, but the person is just being a fool. The evil person is the bull taking direct aim at a person, intent on taking him or her down. The evil person is destructive and intentional.

You may wish to wander down a trail to determine the "Why" behind the evil. You may or may not ever know the answer. Evil people may claim the same excuses used by a foolish person: my terrible childhood, my past abuse, my poverty. But people can become wise and good by changing, taking responsibility for who they are today, and becoming caring and solution oriented. Or they can stay evil.

Don't immerse yourself in discovering why. Be grateful to have a space devoid of them and protect yourself. Cloud quotes the Warren Zevon song about needing "lawyers, guns, and money" to protect yourself.[10]

You do need every tool you can acquire to protect yourself, your sanity, any possessions you have, and any other people you care about. Evil people may wish to destroy you so they don't look so evil. Evil people may want to destroy you financially so they can feel superior. They may want to destroy you so that their incompetence in their job won't be exposed. They may want to destroy just because they're evil.

Identifying a person as evil empowers you to put strict boundaries in place. You can define your space as off-limits, letting the evil person know that coming to your address means you'll call 911 and have him or her removed. (That's the "guns" we have available.) Most of us have little interest in securing lawyers and all that entails. Unfortunately, litigation is sometimes necessary.

I watched in frustration as a young mom I know struggled to see her husband's behavioral indicators for what they really were. Her husband left her and accumulated great debt, using the home she and their daughter lived in as collateral. He had reduced her to personal insecurity until she was unable to keep a job and dependent on his poor choices. It took foreclosure notices for her finally to listen to us. We were holding a light up to the truth of his behavior while she clung to, "But he loved me" and "How could he do this to his daughter?" One-word answer: Evil.

In the greatest book of wisdom, the Bible, we are admonished not even to walk with evil people. Psalm 1:1 tells us, Don't hang around people doing bad things or mocking others. Making fun of others and/or putting them down not only destroys the person doing the mocking but everyone else in their company. *Evil sees* becomes *evil does*. Run, don't walk. This person can destroy you.

START INVESTING YOUR RESOURCES

Remember Albert Einstein's saying that doing the same thing over expecting different results is a sign of insanity? This new void in your life is your opportunity to do something different. You've heard me repeat that we can just stay stuck or Just Start Something. I don't use the phrase "starting over." That implies going back to the starting line—starting the race again on the same old tires and same old life patterns. You already know what the result will be. The same old, same old.

No, this is our chance to start something unique, incorporating the strengths we've gained from our loss. We're embarking on our new beginning, not in spite of our loss but rather because of it. We've been forever changed and are better, wiser, and more courageous for it. While we'll explore this in greater depth in chapter six, let's look at how we can start.

Hudson Taylor described the three stages of anything difficult: Impossible, Difficult, Done.[11] His incredibly challenging life as a missionary in China thrust him into more seemingly impossible places than most of us will ever face. However, those of us starting over because of loss can relate to his description of what we're looking at. From our empty space, starting a new life, a new adventure, looks *impossible.*

An example of impossible I observed was the growing of Macadamia nuts in Baja, California, the Pacific coast of Mexico. As a volunteer there, I just showed up willing to do any task to help a local orphanage. I was given a crowbar one day and assigned to rip roofing off an old building. Fun! The next day I was pruning and grafting Macadamia trees. Interesting! Why were these tasks necessary?

Growing Macadamia trees could help fund the orphanage. Macadamia nuts are valuable. The problem was that the space was near the

Pacific Ocean, where winds are constant and strong. Most Macadamia trees don't thrive in windy locations. A horticulturalist discovered a type of Macadamia tree that loved the soil of the Baja but not the wind. He discovered another type that could handle the wind, but was not fond of the soil. His solution was to plant the soil-loving trees, but prune and graft into them the wind-loving variety. Result: plentiful crops of Macadamia nuts.

In our void we probably feel we can't thrive again, at least not here, or not now, or not for long. It's a good time to consider in what soil we thrive. If we're in that soil and growing, what in our life might need pruning and what needs grafting in? We're now in a space of new options—looking at our life with fresh perspective. What works? What doesn't? What freedoms do we have to make different choices?

Let me illustrate from my family tree. I am one of a sisterhood of four. Typical of divorce statistics, two have experienced that end of a first marriage. Since many of you reading this book may be in that place, let me tell you what I saw in my sisters after their losses. Yes, it describes their living space, but I think you'll see rays of hope from their experience at that time.

They both suffered financially after their divorces. Both tell me that, while the divorce itself was the greatest blow to their sense of being a worthy person, their resulting poverty was one quick follow-up kick. The inclination to believe that their worth depended on either their marital status or their pocketbook simply demanded reconsideration in the devastation. By both of those standards, they were at ground zero.

In time they both came to believe and live by Paul's words: "I know what it is to be in need, and I know what it is to have plenty. I have learned the secret of being content in any and every situation, whether well fed or hungry, whether living in plenty or in want" (Philippians 4:12).

One sister, having moved from a nine-room home to a two-room apartment, became a one-room boarder with kitchen privileges. She struggled to rediscover who she was. Although money was certainly not her idol before, she found it hard to separate what she had been, and where she lived from who she was in that moment.

Since that time we've walked the Hudson Riverside and the trails of Sedona, Arizona. Satisfaction has smoothed the worry lines that tough times had carved on her face. In that empty time she overcame an addiction that had become her crutch during her difficult marriage. She is now grateful for that difficult time, the lessons she learned, and the life-changing, in fact, life-preserving changes she has made. She's mustard-seed strong.

My other sister, in her third year of being on her own, offered me a cup of coffee in her new accommodations. She reached for the coffeepot that sat on top of the refrigerator—the only available spot for it in her new home. One-room studios in converted, old "painted-lady" homes are not known for spacious cabinets or counter space.

I cleared a space on her couch—which also served as her bed—for our tray. Her live-in companion, a ferret who gazed at us as we spoke with an intelligent look as if he understood all we were saying, stood nearby on his hind legs. I believe he fancied himself a human enjoying our conversation. Thank goodness for the familiar plants and ostrich feathers in the window and her unusual choice of pets. I knew she was still herself. Everything changed on the outside, but her love of color, living things, and unique objects remained.

Her bank account may have measured her as poor. But her soul was not poor. Several years later now, she has earned her master's degree in special education and has a career helping four-year-old children with disabilities begin their school years. Her compassion is evident. That empty space in her life became her new beginning to Just Start Something. She is now living on her strengths. I'm sure her students delight in seeing what their gypsy-like teacher will wear each day which usually includes feathers somewhere.

With our wiser eyes, we are probably more aware of the strengths we have. Our weaknesses are probably more visible to us now than they ever were before as well. In our new beginning, we want to build on our strengths. Building on strengths moves us forward. Simply focusing on shoring up our weakness will bring slow progress, if any.

In what settings do we grow well? This is a good time to consider even the dreams we had as a teen. As young adults, what prompted us to study the extra hour, run the extra mile? What were our passions and the desires of our heart?

I love seeing evidence of this truth in nature. I referred earlier to my unwise leap into Crater Lake in Oregon. It is the clearest, cleanest, deepest lake in our country. There are no words to describe the change in its color as the sun magically repaints it throughout the day: lavender, aqua, pale blue, royal, almost black.

What created this natural wonder? Devastation—a volcano erupted, blowing the top off a mountain and leaving death in its wake. The empty crater was lined with lava that would grow no plants and allow no streams from the outside into this gaping hole. The mountain was so high that it rose above where the air was filled with impurities. Result, no plant life falls in to pollute, no dirty rivers dump there. The water is pure and beautiful—because of a volcanic eruption. The final result was purity unmatched in any other lake in our country.

I drank in its beauty and was reminded that God can make beauty from catastrophe.

The result of volcano eruptions don't follow any pattern. The eruption of Mount St. Helen's created a different new beginning. Before we look at that, let's absorb a lesson. As humanoids, we should not compare ourselves to others and how they came through the times of loss in their lives. We're all so different. Remember our masterpiece lessons from chapter two? We are all uniquely made, masterpieces in the present not because of how we look now, but because we're a creation in progress of a masterful Artist. Crater Lake and Mount St. Helen's are quite different today from what they looked like only thirty years ago.

The eruption of Mount St. Helen's is one of our country's most devastating events. Thirty years have passed, and most of us have forgotten the names of those whose lives were lost, the towns that disappeared, the ash that shut down airports, and how life came to a standstill for thousands that dreaded day in May 1980. It was the Northwest's version of 9/11.

As a now-single person rediscovering traveling alone, I decided to take the helicopter ride and flew low over the sight. Miles of brown remain. The gaping hole in the side of a once-lofty mountain is the main monument to the destruction. But farther down the path of the lava flow, a patch of vegetation defies the devastation. Not only has green appeared, a small herd of elk graze as if nothing happened here. I had another real glimpse of God creating beauty from ashes.

We have those moments when we feel life's devastation is irreversible. Grab God's view. He doesn't see it that way.

4

Better: The Blue Bowl Perspective

One of the most precious families I know taught me a valuable lesson. I call it the Big Blue Bowl perspective.

This special family adopted three young boys from extremely disadvantaged backgrounds. At age six and a half, the first son entered their world. Accustomed to hunger and neglect, he was in a family for the first time. He would not need to move again and wonder whether his tiny bag of belongings would still be his or someone else would take them. In a short time, the family brought in two more young boys, one a bit younger than their first and one a bit older. To say the children were malnourished is a tremendous understatement. Tiny arms however could not detract from their shy engaging smile, looks that seemed to inquire, "Is this for real? Will you be staying in my life, or will I soon be saying another good-bye?"

Mama and Papa in this situation began a rigorous, regimented family routine, which, looking on, I thought would be disastrous. Because I regularly spent lots of time with them, which often included meals, barbecues, and just snack time, my thought was that little boys need some ice cream, cookies, and a bit of soda now and then. It's comfort food. But those items were not on the parent-approved menu. The boys ate three balanced meals a day, and each meal included protein, vegetables or fruit, and only whole-grain breads. No cookies, cakes, ice cream, or pop were allowed at their house—or mine either. To me, this spelled trouble at best, or was preposterous at worst. This added deprivation would cause them to have eating disorders later on, if their tough start had not already exacerbated that tendency. Or so I thought.

However, the boys were allowed to eat all day—from anything in the Big Blue Bowl on the kitchen counter. That bowl contained terrible-tasting protein bars with no chocolate chips in them and no marshmallows. The bowl also contained bananas, pears, apples, and raisins. Straw-like, blah-tasting packets of nutritious oat-like stuff were also in the bowl. But the bowl was always available. The boys could have all they wanted.

The schedule was also regimented. Regular bedtime: 8:30 p.m., no exceptions, even during sleepovers at my house. Saturday night was nail trimming, hair trimming, get-looking-your-best time. Weekday wake-up time was one hour earlier than necessary for getting ready for school. The boys spent that hour being tutored in mathematics and language skills to make up for lost opportunity in the early grades in school. No exceptions!

Thank goodness, I complied (which was tough) and restrained myself from speaking my mind (which was even tougher), and looked on.

Weeks became months. The boys' thin arms began to gain muscle. They laughed a lot. Slumping shoulders disappeared. They walked confidently with shoulders back and chests out, looking me directly in the eye with a contagious twinkle. They scampered out the door to school with completed homework in their backpacks.

Having never had the opportunity to be in sports programs or teams, the boys wanted to join any and every sport. The family's back door required special bins for soccer shoes, basketball shoes, flip-flops for swim days, and Sunday shoes.

Years have passed. I now must admit that the Big Blue Bowl was not such a bad idea after all.

The boys' homework now includes studying Mandarin Chinese and French. Wrestling and rugby shoes have replaced those little shoes of yesterday. Athletic medals crowd their bedroom shelves and dresser tops. More importantly, they are young men of character and strength. The Big Blue Bowl is no longer necessary.

What seemed restrictive was actually a new path to thriving after years of loss.

Here's the application: After loss, we are like those little boys. God sets out His Big Blue Bowl. Indulging is allowed. What's in that bowl is what He knows is best for us considering what we've been through.

However, there's a contrast here. We might prefer what I'll call the Sumptuous Silver Bowl. This bowl is full of indulgent stuff like Twinkies, cookies, Mountain Dew, chocolate bars, and other things we might like but are not in our best interests now. In fact, our impulse might even tell us we deserve these indulgences now more than ever, as comfort, given our circumstances. But indulging in the Sumptuous Silver Bowl means we just stay stuck—no moving forward. The Big Blue Bowl is what we need so that we can Just Start Something.

You may feel unable now struggling after your loss to even know what should be in your Big Blue Bowl. There's help for you. Start with listening to the right people.

HELP FROM THE RIGHT PEOPLE

After a significant loss, you need help from wise people—you need a Board of Directors. In fact, you may already have such a board and simply are not aware of them. I developed the concept for my book *From One Widow to Another*. As I shared the concept, people experiencing different losses told me it helped them. In fact, some found the idea life-changing. Putting together this board simply means you'll be selecting wise people to surround you. They will hold a mirror up to who you are now, what you've experienced, and help you face forward. I call these folks your Board of Directors.

Imagine a boardroom with a large, impressive table. High-back chairs surround it. You sit at the head of the table. Each chair represents a person to advise you, to vote on your actions, and bring you information. You listen to these people, whether you wish to or not. They are your VIPs, the movers and shakers of your world, the POIs (people of influence) in your life.

What determines who sits in each chair? Likely two have been, and perhaps still are, your parents. You might invite favorite teachers or relatives to join your board. Life events may result in an unwelcome intruder. If your parents divorced, one parent may have vacated a chair and left a spot for someone not of your choosing to sit down. The newcomer's power over your life may give that person VIP status whether you like it or not.

Take a pad of paper and sketch your table and chairs. Imagine your Board of Directors. Who are they? Label each chair. We typically have one Board of Directors in our youth, determined by our family, culture, and circumstances. But we change and our board members change as we move through the stages of our lives. At one time you may have six chairs at your imaginary table, and in another season you may need fifteen. Not all board members are equally necessary or important to you, but each is a person who matters to you.

Some of us welcome to our table people we have never met. In the graduate school season of my life I devoured the writings of Francis and Edith Schaeffer. As a believer, marriage partner, and mother, I invited Edith to my table. I "listened" to her through her books on faith, family, and hospitality. Because of Edith Schaeffer's presence at my table, Neff hospitality happened in a new and different way.

A director may be from a previous century (through books) or your twin sister. You may not even recognize the importance of these people until you do this exercise!

With each major life event, people change on your board. Some depart willingly; some you have to remove. A new career may bring a new mentor you trust and value. A geographical move combined with a busy schedule may eventually remove a director. Sometimes they just fade away. Given the reality that we are all humanoids—subject to messing up in small and large ways—some of our VIPs misstep, disappoint us, show themselves unfit to sit at our table. Some may leave because they disapprove of our behavior. Their exit may be both understandable and appropriate. The commercial that says, "Life comes at us fast" makes an understatement. The constant flux of a personal Board of Directors reflects that.

And now you have experienced loss. If your loss is your spouse, due to either divorce or death, that spouse who is no longer there in reality is probably influencing you by still sitting on your Board of Directors. Your spouse was a VIP. If he or she was good and wise, input in your life was huge and positive. Even if she or he was unwise, that person may continue to be one of your VIPs for months and years to come. You'll need to work hard to remove that person from the Board of Directors in your brain. You'll need to ignore unwanted messages left in your mind.

> There's something to be said for the person who can relate. Find that person.

Some board members disappear because our friendship networks change through times of loss. We are usually surprised by those who remove themselves from our lives. Those departures might hurt. But life is real; behavior does not lie; and life must go on. That empty chair is a positive opportunity for another valuable individual who cares about you in your current circumstance.

So why go to such lengths to examine who sits at your board? Because you are now facing a great opportunity to choose. With the myriad choices you must now make, this is a good time to evaluate who belongs at your table. In your new circumstance some should be invited to exit.

Let me offer a word of caution. Some of us have discovered that upon our loss, some pull their chairs up to our boardroom table uninvited. I have seen children, not just adult children but sometimes younger children, become the movers and shakers, influencing a parent in the season after loss and not always in a good way.

The months and years after a significant loss is a key time to take advantage of our changing world. We can evaluate and select a wise board for the challenges we face.

May I suggest six people you need at your table? You may have many more. These are actually positions with a function that need to be fulfilled in your new life. The list is in no particular order, and some individuals may even fill two positions.

Board Member 1: A godly person who has experienced a similar loss

The power of a similar connection is the basis for support groups, mentoring relationships, and strength beyond measure. While I have not experienced the death of a child, my friends who have tell me there is no greater comforter or one who can help you through it like another parent who has lost a child. Before I became a widow, I would never have imagined the value of another widow in my life. Would not any wise person who has experienced loss be helpful? Not really. There's a special connection created when you look directly into the eyes of someone who has shared something similar. That look says, "I understand."

This is especially true when someone you love is incarcerated. Those who have had to remove their shoes and all other belongings, get searched, and go through three sets of gates in order to look into the eyes of someone they love—they understand your pain. Their hug of comfort is real, and their words are wise.

Of course, no two losses are exactly alike. Even if they were quite similar, our personal differences, personalities, and past experiences mean our journeys will be at least a bit different. But there's something to be said for the person who can relate. Find that person. It may be through a support group or even through blogs on the Internet as well as community resources.

The person who has experienced a similar loss will understand your particular vulnerability and be able to let you know what he or she most needed in a Big Blue Bowl. And, we hope, this board member will be transparent enough to tell you the Sumptuous Silver Bowl indulgences that didn't help him or her so you can avoid that pitfall.

Board Member 2: A person with financial wisdom

This person is incredibly important in your boardroom. There are few losses that initially add resources to our lives. Typically, loss means revising our expenditures, usually downward—not an easy task, especially when we're hurting and vulnerable to making poor decisions. If it's a job loss in a declining career market, we may have more time but few help lines to point us in a direction that leads to another job.

We do need to have an informed voice at our table who "gets it" when it comes to managing resources God has given us for our provision. Of course, this person needs to be committed to confidentiality and to managing his or her own finances well.

Communities and churches often offer workshops that can be quite helpful. Don't wait to find this person. They can't and shouldn't make your decisions for you, but they can recommend. And it's a good time to listen.

In addition to being creative with financial resources, this board member needs to be willing to speak truth to you. One family, after a great financial loss, wisely went for financial counseling. The counselor identified that they spent large sums on gifts at Christmastime. Though the counselor pointed out that this was no longer a wise practice, the family rejected that advice. They insisted that Christmas wouldn't be Christmas without the elaborate gifts—that's just how they did it! How sad! Their financial decline continued to take a toll on their credit and their future, while it strained the parents' relationship.

While your finance board member may have financial advising credentials, that is not necessary. If you want such a person, check credentials, interview at least three, and be willing to change if that person doesn't seem best for you in this season of your life.

If a person is worth inviting to your boardroom, listen carefully to his or her wisdom. You may choose to just stay stuck or Just Start Something. If financial independence and living within a balanced budget are not already a reality, those are the places to start.

Board Member 3: A practical friend

You and I are capable of straight thinking. We can and will navigate all these changes. We can figure it out. But this might not be the moment that straight thinking is our strong suit. Common sense is, well, *uncommon* when we're struggling with loss. I understand.

Especially in those early months, it is good to have someone just to be another pair of eyes, other listening ears. Sometimes fear or grief clouds our vision, and we do not see options available to us. We may have a good solution to a problem and just need someone to affirm that.

If you've experienced divorce, this practical friend can give you feedback if you decided to navigate a new relationship. Accountability is a precious gift. In our widows groups both young and vintage have opportunities to date again. Yes, we quiz each other and can help detect that person who is looking for diversion, a paycheck, or a caretaker—all bad foundations for a new relationship. Any person who is single again is at risk for a second marriage that is unlikely to succeed. Statistics speak. This person on your Board of Directors should look objectively at those new relationships.

Practical friends can spot "I don't care" signs that spell trouble for taking care of our living space, and more importantly taking care of our health. Again, these practical friends need to be courageous enough to speak the truth, and we need to be open to listening.

Board Member 4: An encourager

Count yourself blessed if you have one person in your life who encourages you, believes in you, and always expects the best of you. This is a good time to lean heavily in this friend's direction and soak up that affirmation. Research shows that people actually move through the grieving process faster with a supportive network around them.

You'd think that surrounding ourselves with encouragers would be natural, a no-brainer. However, I have observed literally the opposite. Humanoids are capable of, in their time of loss and badly needing encouragement, linking up with other floundering people who actually pull them down further. I hope you aren't in this self-destructive place, but it's possible.

If you are in a bad relational place and have been in a negative relationship for some period of time, likely that person has either convinced you or contorted your view of yourself to believe that you are negative, unworthy, maybe even a throwaway person. Even if they have abandoned and/or divorced you, you accept their version of you.

I have observed, up close and personal, that beaten-down person rejecting available counsel or encouragement and avoiding the freedom to move on. Humanoids can be so desperately duped and brainwashed that they reject any encouragement. Pointing out any good characteristics they have or might have had at one time is a wasted effort. They repeat the negative line they have been listening to for years. Likely these people have come to believe that another person's problems are their fault as well. If you struggle with self-perception and accepting encouragement, take some time to review the differences between foolish and wise people charted in chapter three, looking for the behavioral indicators that will help you gain insights. You might even have your encouraging board member help you think it through.

You may be inclined to accept untruths about yourself and not realize it. Here are a few questions to ask yourself that may hold up the *real* mirror: *Are there people you are refusing to talk to because you assume you know what they'll say, and you don't want to hear it? Is it possible that you'd be the wiser for at least listening?*

One such person would only listen to people who encouraged him to stay in a negative relationship with a person who had already left him in every way except for existing in the same living space. He was saddened that no one was "encouraging" him. It was clear to everyone except himself that it was time for him to move on.

There are people who will have your best interests at heart. If they've distanced themselves from you, it might be because there's only one thing you want to hear and they love you too much to tell you that lie.

Think of those people you know who are positive and have been positive in your past. Reach out, reconnect, and let those positive people draw up a chair at your boardroom table.

Board Member 5: A person with spiritual discernment and courage

Having a spiritual mentor is a gift—a rare one, I believe. Successful businessmen often have mentors to help navigate and even create their mobile path upward. Athletes have coaches. Chefs learn under master chefs. Pastors are usually paired with spiritual leaders. Personal trainers are popular among people seeking healthy lifestyles. So why should not we who desire a growing spiritual life seek out our own trainers, coaches, or mentors?

As you consider which friends fulfill this function in your life, remember, in order for them to occupy chairs at the table for your Board of Directors, they need to have some level of understanding of *you*. You need to be able to glean from them information relevant to *your* life. That means you must trust them enough to be transparent. If they don't know your temptations, they can't advise you specifically where and when you need advice.

We have all seen spiritual leaders stumble and sometimes fall. In one particularly public failure, I knew several people of spiritual depth and discernment who lived nearby and would have been willing and capable mentors for that leader. They had no idea the path of destruction their neighbor was on.

Finding this board member might require more searching than filling the other boardroom chairs, but the right person needs to occupy that important chair. Leaving this chair empty is simply unwise.

Board Member 6: A relative whose priority is your well-being

If you are the kind of person who gravitates to reading the advice columns in magazines and newspapers (I'm one of those), you know that many advice seekers are at least puzzled, if not provoked, by the behavior of a relative. We married more than a man or a woman. We married a branch of a family, and in that union we grafted into our tree some branches occupied by strange and wonderful birds. And while we're being real here, let's admit that some relatives are south of strange.

I have learned from my ministry, Widowconnection.com, that widows' living circumstances come in all shapes and sizes, ages and families, wrapped in expectations from their culture, and baggage (both heavy and uplifting) from their marriages. Rarely is a widow totally alone. The family tree certainly changes when a husband dies, and we must adjust to that reality.

This truth applies when divorce severs a branch from the family tree. The limbs of cousins, aunts and uncles, grandparents, and step-relatives shake in the gusting winds.

I've observed that one family member's financial change shakes the whole family tree. If there is huge loss, some relatives boast that they saw it coming. Some distance themselves fearing they will be called on to help. Financial gain is likely to bring a new flock of bird relatives to the tree— ones you never knew belonged.

Family members usually react to your loss. During a time when emotions are intense and maybe even deceptive, that relative who is level-headed and communicates clearly can be the advocate we need. While relatives can be challenging, we are usually better off if we don't isolate ourselves from everyone.

The exception is that really strange bird who is difficult at best to relate to, even in good times. This is not your good time. Giving yourself a break from expected contacts with that relative is not only appropriate while you heal and restore, it's wise.

Before we leave this important topic of getting help from wise people, here's another example that has helped me know who I need surrounding me. We need to know what people can bring, given their positive influence as we move forward.

At the same time I was healing from the greatest loss in my life, I was moving forward to begin an organization to help others who had experienced that same loss. At times I wanted to turn back the hands of time. At other times I was eager to forge ahead in the totally new adventure of starting a ministry. This meant incorporating a business, securing not-for-profit status, and starting the work that was so badly needed.

As I researched and sought advice from experts both in person and through books and articles, I began to notice a significant fact: Frequently new start-up companies and new ministries and missions are launched by people who have experienced loss or even a crisis. Reading their backgrounds, I noticed that some had experienced failure that resulted in a bright idea with potential to help themselves and others based on what they learned from that failure. Others, like me, had experienced a loss and found no resources to help.

The previous loss or perceived failure left a void, a void these people determined to fill with a solution. This may be true for you as well. You might not see it in this moment. But just the recognition that others have used that void to move into a positive opportunity is worth noting. Others have managed to Just Start Something.

I'll share a bit of my journey because I experienced the value of having an excellent Board of Directors to help me personally. That, in turn, was a good foundation for starting something new.

 Simple is better in most areas of life.

Our vision to help widows propelled Widow Connection on a growth curve. I found out that when God gives us not only an assignment but a passion for one of His causes, things happen! In learning about how to grow an organization wisely, I was advised by a mentor to make sure we got the right people on the bus. Some folks will do great on another bus, not ours. This friend and international leader elaborated. Each person on the bus needs to be in the right seat. Seats marked "technical," "creative," "visionary," or "detail oriented" need appropriate people wired up with those different gifts. The right person in the wrong seat is still a disaster. His final reminder: Sometimes people need to get off the bus—sooner rather than later.

This friend's bus metaphor applies to our Board of Directors as well. Just because we have a relative at the table who helps us navigate the relative stuff doesn't mean that same person is qualified to advise us in financial matters. Practical people may not have the spiritual stature to hold us accountable on character issues. Those people who are so helpful personally may not be business mentors if you are Just Starting Something. You need to pick a different crew for that adventure.

In my case, my business/ministry mentors needed to be the right fit for these questions: Are they all out for this mission? Do they get the James 1:27 mandate? "Religion that God our Father accepts as pure and faultless is this: to look after orphans and widows in their distress and to keep oneself from being polluted by the world." Are these mentors occupying the right seats? Do their skill sets match their job descriptions? If they're on the bus, and the relationship is not working, don't wait to replace them. Why is this good advice that works? Because it's biblical.

Jesus' team was intentionally selected. Others wanted to follow Him but didn't embrace His whole mission. And Jesus spent time apart alone with God in prayer before picking His people. One might question the diversity and unique selections Jesus made for His twelve disciples. However, consider the results. Jesus invested only three years in training, mentoring, and leading by example. Then He left the disciples on their own. And they became the continuing catalyst that changed the world.

God selected Moses to do a big job, knowing well Moses' weaknesses and strengths. Moses had to grow into his new responsibilities. Yes, there's discomfort in growth. But in the new adventure I'm on, the discomfort is balanced by the reality that my work is His mandate, His ministry. I may be the driver, but He's the engine.

The right people in the right seats matter. Proverbs 15:22 says, "Plans fail for lack of counsel, but with *many advisers* they succeed" (emphasis mine).

HELP FROM THE RIGHT STUFF

Did you notice that the Big Blue Bowl was filled with simple things? Most of us discover after loss that not only do we not want to juggle extra stuff, we simply can't. When Ginger, who you met in chapter one, pared down her six children's toy and game supply so they could move to a tiny apartment, she discovered that her children did not suffer from toy deprivation. Their wardrobes are trimmed to bare bones as well, which actually makes the morning "get ready" time easier.

One couple who lost their dream home to foreclosure discovered that not having the elaborate exercise room did not keep them from staying in shape. They vigorously walk around their new neighborhood and are getting to know each other better. Their walk provides conversation time they seldom had in their life before. Little had they realized how much time they were spending maintaining their stuff, from home to cars to wardrobes.

Simple is better in most areas of life. Eating habits and food costs are yoked inseparably. How often do we read that fruits, vegetables, grains, and protein are healthier the less they are processed? Refining, canning, preserving often removes some value and adds some costs. For most of us, we have to adjust to thinking ahead a bit more. Fresh produce in season costs less, though that January strawberry sure looks good. Picking up produce ahead of time so we're not tempted to stop for fast food—which costs more money and is less nutritious—requires planning. But we experience loads of contentment as we realize we're getting more value for our investment and being kinder to ourselves and our bodies as well.

Try something different. You may be amazed that you feel a fresh boost of energy simply from that change.

Don't be discouraged by the effort it takes to simplify. The rewards are huge! You'll look back and see your simpler life as a great benefit and blessing that was the result of your loss.

While my frequent trips to Africa are focused on helping widows, I've found that those travels continue to draw me to a more simple life. My first stay in a village with no electricity taught me beautiful lessons. Life can be delightful with no nightlife. Darkness means sleep; there's nothing else to do—except, of course, to walk out of your hut, gaze up, and see the most dazzling display of stars you've ever seen.

The only inconvenience was a solvable problem. I had not considered the fact that I always need light to remove my contacts for the night. Darkness came. I hadn't thought of that. *What to do, what to do?* I remembered seeing a pickup truck parked near the kitchen structure. I made my way there, stepping carefully. A kindly looking gentleman and several women were still sitting around a fire. Using sign language since I speak neither Portuguese nor the local dialect, I pointed to the truck and to my eyes. Staring blankly at me (probably no one in that village has ever worn contacts), they seemed puzzled. The gentleman nodded and pointed to the truck.

I clambered in, turned on the rooftop light, and extracted my contacts into their holder. Pushing my glasses on my nose, I smiled, waved, and walked back to my hut. At dusk the next day, I'd remove my contacts.

Every time I return home after a trip to Africa and confront the trappings of my household, I realize anew that less is more. Sorting, donating, recycling happens after each visit.

In chapter three, we looked at the dangers of hoarding as a way to fill some voids after loss. Applying the Big Blue Bowl concept, we can focus on feasting continually, as needed, on what we need most. So what do we need around us that actually adds value to our lives? We begin to evaluate things and pastimes. Is it necessary? Is it helpful? Have we moved it around more than we've used it? Maybe it's the right stuff—for someone else.

HELP FROM THE RIGHT STRUCTURES

This period after a loss is a good time to evaluate the structures you've developed in your life. How are they working for you today? A daily routine that worked well for you in a past season may not work so well for you today. We are such creatures of habit, sometimes we hang on to the old structures of life without taking the time to be sure they're still wise and helpful.

If your loss has been an important person in your life, no doubt your daily routine was influenced by that person. That person's participation in your life influenced the places you went, the food you shopped for, how you spent your days. And now that person is gone.

With any bit of extra energy you can muster, intentionally revise your daily routine and try something different. You may be amazed that you feel a fresh boost of energy simply from that change.

If your loss has been a result of career upheaval, a daily routine that revolved around a former job and its responsibilities is now defunct. You may be restructuring days of job searching, or adjusting to a new job that wouldn't have been your first choice. Look for the perks and blessings that accompany the new pattern of your days. Change can feel good, with the freshness of a new beginning. Empty hours can be an opportunity to walk, swim, and become more active—and a great way to reduce stress.

Is there an especially difficult hour in your day when you feel your loss more strongly? Maybe that's the moment to add something new. What would you enjoy that you never had time for before? Maybe that lonely late afternoon time is a time to read. Whether you pick up a novel, travelogue, or spiritual encouragement, let your mind go to a new place. If waking up to an empty living space is painful, make that moment your time to step outside and walk, or even run.

No one else can pick that different thing for you. But we do know that clinging to a life structure that served you before might not be so great today.

It has been said that necessity is the mother of invention. This is your time to invent a new routine. The human mind knows no limits to finding ways to "make do," as we'd say in southern Indiana.

One illustration from my childhood was the ever-changing family menu. Drought, too much rain, and insects played havoc with our garden. And we ate only what we produced on the farm. With the practical wisdom that only farm families have, the family could see the problem coming. For example, our lush Concord grapevines were the source of jams, pies, and fresh fruit. One year it became apparent that, unless weather conditions improved, the grapes would rot before they ripened. As a result, we ate green grape pie—that is, "not ripe green grape pie."

At times there were no lemons available. We ate vinegar pie (definitely not my favorite). Rust was setting in on the tomato plants and we knew they'd never have the chance to ripen. The result? Fried green tomatoes! Now that's a tasty dish.

Necessity stimulates creative thinking.

The Maasi people of Kenya typically are barefoot. But we noticed many wearing flip-flop-like sandals made of strips of old tires. Footwear created from the materials at hand, they were quite comfortable and probably would last a decade. I brought home a pair that will undoubtedly outlast any sandals I own.

So you see, you'll probably have fresh and wonderful ideas in this season of your life—not in spite of your loss but because of it.

Jerry Sittser makes an important point in his book *A Grace Disguised: How the Soul Grows Through Loss.* He points out that recovery after loss is impossible. What's possible is discovery.[12] Our response is of supreme importance, and that response determines our future. I agree. As we said in chapter one, you can't have IT back, whatever it is you've lost. The loss changes us. If IT were to reappear in our lives—that person, that career, that job, that home, that thing—we would be so changed by the experiences of our loss that our new day would not be a day of recovery. We wouldn't have back what we had. The change within us would mean our new day would be a day of discovery.

Here are some possible discoveries.

A marriage more treasured.
A child more loved and enjoyed.
A home more cared for.
A friendship with more time for just being, not doing.
A job not taken for granted.
A career with more intentional attention.
A business with more focus on the important.

The list could be endless, diverse. Our point is that recovery of what's been lost might be a realistic expectation of a stolen or misplaced object, but not a life event, not the loss of a relationship. However, even when recovery is out of the question, discovery is always a possibility.

Romans 12:2 provides insight for our options: "Do not conform to the pattern of this world, but be transformed by the renewing of your mind." We can be conformed by our past, restricted by our loss—or we can be transformed, changed. We can be shackled or crushed by our past or remade, remixed, and renewed. To be renewed is to have a fresh life of strength or even replacement. That's a world apart from being conformed to who we were before our loss. It's our choice.

As you sort through this time of change remember that the changed person you'll become is like no one else. You may learn from watching others, seeking their wisdom, even following in someone else's footsteps for a while. But the transformed new you will be unlike any other person.

I started this chapter with the story of three little boys and their Big Blue Bowl experience. One of them illustrated to me another of God's truths. One Sunday afternoon, my husband and I played Dominos with the boys while their dad snoozed on the floor with the Sunday papers strewn around him. Their mom headed off to a nearby department store to buy much-needed winter coats for the oncoming cold—their first winter in the family.

She returned with her bundles. It was time for the boys to try on the winter gear so Mom could decide if the items were keepers or not. The youngest was first and thoughtfully donned a beautiful royal blue jacket with hood. He looked in the mirror. With his dark skin and black eyes, no young man could have looked more handsome.

"Who wore this before?" he questioned.

First my heart broke. He had never owned clothing that had not been someone else's first, and he might be even second or third. Then I listened.

"Oh, honey," his mom answered. "No one. See the tags are still on it. It's new just for you!"

A broad smile expanded over his whole face. He squared his shoulders and turned sideways in the mirror. This new blue jacket was just for him and him alone.

So you're looking forward and wondering what you'll be putting on in this season of life and change. God has a new jacket for you, and it's uniquely yours, designed for just you. No one has worn it before. You'll be a masterpiece in it, because the Master designed both you and what's ahead in your new life.

What structures might you change in order to be transformed?

Examine your daily routine and habits. What repeatedly keeps you rehashing the past? That needs to go. Reminders can even be clothing, places you shop, or room scents. Remember my friend who, when she became single again, missed the social dining-out events she had enjoyed before? Instead of sitting around morosely, she called friends who shared her interest in classical music and invited them to events they would all enjoy. Another friend started a Sunday Supper Soup-or-Salad Club. They rotated between living spaces, each bringing a simple dish to share.

Consider what you feed your body. Transformation takes energy, an unlikely possibility if our body is continually depleted with taking in the wrong stuff or the wrong amounts. Allowing rest is a good thing. However, beware of too much sleep as a form of denial, a way to avoid living the reality of the day.

Consider what you feed your soul. Spiritual nourishment that was adequate before this season of loss may not be enough for now. If you find it difficult to read, music may be the medium through which you can be reminded of God, His goodness, and the fact that He's still there for you.

Consider and evaluate those people in whom you invest your time. Some folks are "Hard Times" magnets. You probably know what I mean. They are at their favorite stride when they come alongside other folks in their struggles. But some of these "helpers" only help that fellow struggler to wallow and waste rather than helping the struggler rise and renew. Find new folks to hang out with! You don't need "Hard Times" magnets now.

GRATITUDE

Would you like to know the not likely but *guaranteed* source of transformation? This is so simple, you might dismiss it. Don't. Stay with me here.

Be grateful.

You might say, "I can't! I just don't feel thankful." Being grateful is not just a feeling. More importantly, it's a discipline.

The feeling of gratitude comes easily when good things happen. But that gratitude is fleeting. When good things come to you easily and quickly without much effort, the feeling of gratitude is even more short-lived.

The discipline of gratitude is a different matter. To have wished for, put every ounce of effort to, pinned your hopes and dreams on, and then bet the farm on that one thing—and then to receive it—that gratitude runs deep and long.

There's a greater, deeper gratitude still. It's gratitude chiseled from what we did not ask for, gratitude for something we had *not* perceived as a wished-for life requirement. This gratitude comes when we look about us at all we do not have. We know very well what we did not get, even though we longed for it. In fact the landscape at that moment is like the charcoal scape of Death Valley, or the wilderness in Israel, or the Sahara desert. We don't see a thing to be grateful for. That is when practicing the discipline of gratitude is most precious, rewarding, and transforming.

One writer challenged his readers to list one thousand things they were thankful for. Don't start with that large a goal. But start somewhere.

By looking for that one tiny thing to be thankful for, you are sending a signal to your entire being that you are not bound by the present and that the best is yet to come. I introduced two young widows to each other. We were practicing gratitude that day. One husband had died due to a three-year battle with cancer. The other had been lost in a tragic, sudden accident. Both women were single-parenting young children, not an easy task. One was grateful they had time to say goodbye; the other was grateful that there was no long period of suffering and pain. They were each making a choice in their circumstances, choosing gratitude.

Gratitude wears different faces.

When the apostle Paul was writing letters in prison, he began each with gratitude. He might conclude with his wish to visit his friends in person, but he started with gratitude, which was not contingent on his gaining freedom.

So my widowed friends found things to be thankful for, even in the midst of their suffering. Something as traumatic as being fired or downsized could even be an opportunity to find something new to be grateful for. A DUI conviction that took your freedom to drive could be the source of gratitude, if only just to be grateful that you will not take someone's life or maim yourself by driving. Gratitude.

It's OK not to be grateful for that bad thing, terrible illness, or tragedy. But it's OK to look around and see what is good—even though what you find to be thankful for seems simple and insignificant to those around you—and be grateful.

Your gratitude might change the people around you. Those who live in a "glass half-empty" world, wallowing deliciously in negativity, won't want to be around you. They'll keep their distance, and that's a good thing. Those who see the glass half-filled will love your company, draw closer, and become your new friendship network. You'll discover they add delicious refreshment to your glass rather than drain it.

Hebrews chapter eleven is the Hall of Fame for humans who seemingly lost all that was important in their lives. And their names are recorded in Scripture as being such great human beings that this earth was not worthy of their presence. God had something better for them and something better for us.

These heroes of faith were the essence of living doing the right thing, no matter what. Their strength was their faith. They were living and dying for something far more important than this earth's goodies and pleasures.

And because of them, we witness living that is otherworldly. We read that they saw beyond the moment, something we learn to do in our time of loss.

Since we're exercising a rare discipline of gratitude when things are bleak, let's look at a reason to be persistent. Hebrews chapter twelve begins by saying we have a cloud of witnesses watching us—a *cloud*, not a handful. These are those who have already finished the human race. They are already present with the Lord (2 Corinthians 5:8). That cloud may also include angels.

This is a reason to be grateful! We're not alone! A persistent temptation in our time of loss is to feel totally alone. It feels as if no one knows and maybe no one cares—at least not much anyway. Wrong! A cloud of witnesses hovers over us wanting to see us transformed, taking on the next lap of our race, grasping that baton no matter how battered and bent it is. As we lean into our next lap, they are cheering us on.

Don't you imagine that among that cloud there are hundreds, maybe thousands, who relate more to what you have gone through than anyone here on earth? And they have another perspective beyond any we can fathom while we're on earth. They are in the presence of our Lord, Creator, and Savior. They KNOW what He can do.

From their perspective they might be saying this about one young mother's desperate situation: "Yes, Lorna, we see you caring, comforting, mothering your disabled little boy who will never talk or run. We see your anticipatory grief that his life will be so short. We sense the yearning of your heart for *normal*, something neither of you will experience on earth. But you can't imagine the comfort of being in Jesus' arms here. Your little boy will experience that sooner rather than later. He'll never enter another hospital or struggle to move forward. He'll never utter a sound that you struggle to understand. He'll be whole here. We're cheering you on! Love him until he gets to us! And there's more. Our Jesus will heal your broken heart. Yes, on earth you'll always bear that scar of the loss of all you hoped your son would be. But there are NO scars here. You would not believe what Jesus can do."

You've got a cloud of witnesses to cheer you on, too.

So, my friend, start simply. Start that list. Write that one thing that you can be grateful for in the moment. Keep the list handy. Keep adding to the list. When your focus has changed to "What can I be grateful for?" you'll be amazed at how your view changes. In fact, why not find a Big Blue Bowl and put it in a visible place. Place in that bowl your sketch of the boardroom you imagined with the names of your possible, selected directors. Add another note with the changes in stuff and structures you'd like to make. And then put in your gratitude list.

You'll treasure what you took for granted, appreciate simplicity, and be transformed.

5

Forgiveness: More Than Recommended, It's Required

It is likely that the place where you are today is a space that you never thought would be *your* space. Surprises and change have landed you here. I call this your Now House because it is your reality today. Before your unwanted change, you may never have imagined such a place existed. Your life before loss was possibly sheltered with some security and predictability. Maybe these were at times shaky, but at least it was space you knew. We'll call this your Before House.

Yet loss has caused you to pick up this book. As we've already said, all losses are different. At the same time, all losses have similarities. We share the common experience of a "Before House." Our Before Houses had daily routines, living spaces, and people in our lives for a host of reasons, some positive and some negative. We had material means, either large or small, that were the basis for our lifestyle. That lifestyle might have been short-sighted and unrealistic, or practical and sustainable. Regardless, that was the trajectory we were on—our routine, our pattern.

Now something has drastically changed. We've been gently nudged or maybe even drop-kicked out of the "Before House." We're in a new room we never knew existed. We know we must adjust, reorganize our lives, and change. We dare in our bold moments to think ahead and wonder what our future will be. Sometimes we can barely think about tomorrow and what that new day may bring. We're just making it through the day in our "Now House."

Our Now House is occupied with the necessities of today. Sometimes it seems that more than twenty-four hours are required just to exist. Ordinary tasks take longer because our surroundings are strange. Intense emotions drain us and drag our actions down to slow motion. You'd think there would be no room for painful memories. Not true.

The "Now House" sometimes is crowded with memories surrounding our loss. And many of those memories have to do with what caused the loss. "Why?" questions pour in.

Just when we think there's no more room for more memories, the what-ifs rush in. Our Now House is now so crowded with congestion from memories, and "Why" and "What if" that we feel immobilized. Can you relate?

Chapter one dealt with moving on from the what-ifs and why questions, addressing them, learning from the past, and moving forward. In our Now House there's more we can do to make sure this place is temporary, a place for a positive transition to what's next.

Don't berate yourself when your mind gets preoccupied with these memories and questions; it is normal for our minds to go to those places. What if that real estate law had not changed? What if the bleeding ulcer happened at home rather than on a cruise ship without appropriate medical support? Our minds can get stuck there. Usually someone or something could have been different or made a difference.

These are not just theoretical examples. Our friend's legal career involved a partnership based on real estate. They were moving and shaking their way to the top in every way including wealth. And then one simple change in real estate law reduced them to financial ruin. This dedicated dad and family man, Christ-follower, and hard worker never recovered. His family never lived the dream they initially began to experience.

Marie and her family decided to celebrate their twentieth wedding anniversary with a cruise including extended family. Thirty family members, including their two teenage children, embarked on the dream cruise of a lifetime. What began as a simple bleeding ulcer incident on the ship became deadly. Airlifted to a nearby island where the hospital was ill-equipped, Marie's husband literally bled to death unnecessarily.

When my friend Ginger's husband was first indicted, the family expected that he'd get a slap on the wrist and not serve prison time. And then the Enron debacle angered everyone, and laws were revised accordingly. That slap on the wrist became a smackdown, causing Ginger to become a single parent for the duration of his prison sentence.

In each of these cases, I've listened as that precious person in each of those circumstances attempted to explain, sort through, make sense of the event that moved them from their Before House into their Now House.

While Marie still lives in the home she and her husband shared, brought their babies home to, and celebrated life in, she says today, "I'd live in a tin can to have him back." Memories can be monopolizing.

"Why?" enters, is mulled over, and exits. And then it intrudes again. "What if" slithers in to be contemplated, drawing one into an unrealistic dreamworld. And then the phone rings, the alarm buzzes. And the necessities of the day push back the memories for the moment.

We know at some level that the Now House is temporary, and we must move toward the Next House. Though we may be exhausted and confused, our human spirit rejects stagnation, and we desire to move forward—even if that means three steps forward and then two steps back.

There is one common necessary event that must occur in every person in their Now House if they want their Next House to be the best it can be: that event is forgiveness.

THE FIRM FOUNDATION
FOR THE NEXT HOUSE

If you think forgiveness is optional, I will tell you tenderly that you are right—if you don't want your Next House to be the best that it can be.

If you think forgiveness can be partial, that you can forgive some people, not others, or that you can forgive part of what others did, but not all, you are right again—if you don't desire that your Next House be the best that it can be.

If you claim that forgiveness is beyond you, given how terribly you've been hurt, you may be right again. However, there is Someone who can help anyone forgive anything. To accept that the power to forgive is beyond you and you won't access that power from the One who can bring forgiveness is your choice—if you don't desire that your Next House be the best that it can be.

What matters is what you want in your Next House.

Forgiveness is neither cheap nor easy. If it were, we'd embrace forgiving people—medical personnel, lawmakers, organizations, human resource departments, decision makers in insurance companies, and politicians. And this is just a partial list. If all of us were to start listing all the possible contributors to our loss, there would be no notebook, either hard copy or electronic, that could contain it. Just making the list would impact our Next House. That list would be useless *unless* we applied forgiveness to every person, event, or organization.

Until the reality of our loss is faced, processed, and forgiven, our future possibilities are restricted.

Let's look at forgiveness and its value. I hope to convince you that if you choose not to forgive, you'll never have the Next House that is the best it can be. I hope to convince you that you *can* forgive, even if you don't feel that it's possible at the moment. I hope to convince you that you have everything to gain and nothing more that really matters to lose if you are willing to forgive.

What's at stake? Your forgiveness of everybody touches a larger circle of people and forces than you can imagine. Those around you see that you have a choice to be bitter, angry, and resentful. You may have a "right" to those feelings, but are those feelings "right" for you? Your attitude, good or bad, is infectious and contagious. Your choice to forgive means those looking on or just touching the periphery of your life will see a person at peace focusing on good in the future rather than the garbage of the past. It's true that forgiveness benefits others. And there are more people in your circle of contacts and influence than you can imagine who will be positively impacted by your act of forgiveness. They are a good reason to forgive.

But there's a good even greater than the good to those around you. Forgiveness will benefit *you*. Forgiveness will refresh your mind, rejuvenate your body, and restore your soul. It will shorten your time in this Now House, and be the foundation for your Next House being the best that it can be. We'll explore each of these benefits to your personal well-being. But the greatest reason of all to forgive is still to come.

Forgiveness brings the greatest good because its outcome and the results of forgiveness are beyond any earthly measure or predictable result. Because forgiving is the right thing to do, our great Creator brings good things to us and to others beyond anything we could cause or imagine. Forgiveness will bring such blessing into your life, and a wealth of such richness, that you'll wonder why anyone would choose not to forgive.

WHAT IS FORGIVENESS?

Let's begin by understanding what forgiveness is and what it is not. Our dictionaries give us a common definition.

Forgiveness is typically defined as the process of concluding resentment, indignation, or anger as a result of a perceived offense, difference or mistake, or ceasing to demand punishment or restitution.[13] The Oxford English Dictionary defines forgiveness as "to grant free pardon and to give up all claim on account of an offense or debt."[14]

These few words are profound. Whether the offense is real or perceived, forgiveness grants free pardon. Whether the offense is real or perceived, forgiveness gives up all claims resulting from that offense.

Forgiveness is a process. At its conclusion we've given up resentment, indignation, and anger.

Let's start by clarifying that if your loss includes legal ramifications for which you are due restitution, forgiving does not preclude you from pursuing what is just. Scripture is clear that taking advantage of anyone who is vulnerable will have consequences. Scripture provides specific examples regarding widows, who are supposed to receive justice and have their grievances heard and addressed. Just because someone can get away with wrongdoing and hurt another in the moment doesn't mean that's the last chorus and verse. There are examples both in the Old Testament and the New that clarify the process of restitution for loss. God declares Himself the Defender of the defenseless. And He's more than good at it.

Your involvement in a legal restitution process has both positives and negatives. If your loss entitles you to financial return, that settlement might obviously help you in your Next House. However, it's not uncommon for that process to be lengthy and require you to stay in your Now House longer than you'd wish, waiting for a verdict.

The website Widowconnection.com receives emails from many young widows whose husband's accidental deaths result in months of legal proceedings, depositions, and investigations. It's not uncommon for that young widow to say that she'd gladly move on with nothing, but cannot for the sake of her children and the support that she needs to continue to be their sole provider and parent.

All these moving parts, including legal proceedings, certainly influence the process of forgiveness. It's important that we not compare and judge who seems to be moving faster or slower through that process.

It's not uncommon for us to forgive at one moment and feel at peace—until another reminder or unknown fact surfaces. The spirit of forgiveness flies out the window and we are once again struggling with anger and turmoil at the wrong of the loss we have suffered. Thankfully, as Christ followers, we can lean into Jesus' words in Matthew 18:21–22 where He answers that we should not only forgive seven times, but seventy times seven.

He knows that we are humanoids, and one time might not be enough. We've forgiven what we knew at the moment, and then more facts and emotions surface. With my husband's untimely death to ALS, I had forgiveness work to do and waded through that arriving at a place of freedom and peace. Insurance companies who initially refused to cover their responsibilities, organizations focusing on how to minimize their input rather than follow policies, folks in the treatment plan with no understanding of the disease—my list was long. And then new information about ALS surfaced that connected its incidence with the many vaccinations men received when they entered the military at the time of the Viet Nam conflict. Bob was one of those men. I had more forgiving to do.

In Scripture, the number seven carries the meaning of completeness and totality. When Jesus tells His followers to forgive 490 times, He means to keep on forgiving, more times than you can count. That's good to know. My friend, you may have reason to forgive repeatedly and for a long time. And you can.

Let's look at the benefits of forgiveness for our health. Studies show that people who forgive are happier and healthier than those who hold resentments. One study that looked at how forgiveness improves physical health discovered that when people think about forgiving an offender it leads to improved functioning in their cardiovascular and nervous systems.[15] Imagine that. Just to begin thinking about forgiving the offender improves the functioning of your heart and your nervous systems. Do you want to be less on edge and less irritable? Just think about forgiving.

Another study at the University of Wisconsin found the more forgiving people were, the less they suffered from a wide range of illnesses. The less forgiving people reported a greater number of health problems.[16] One study identified that those who were taught how to forgive become less angry, feel less hurt, and are more optimistic.[17] Anger is certainly a common emotion in our Now House. Anger summons up adrenaline, which demands action. The energy of adrenaline can be used to do something positive or destructive. Doing nothing but letting anger lie churns our stomachs and denies us sleep. That's why Scripture advises us in Ephesians 4:26 that we make a plan of what to do with our anger by nightfall. Otherwise the refreshment of sleep will be beyond us.

A study from Stanford University also showed that people who forgive in one set of circumstances become more forgiving in a variety of situations, and become more compassionate and self-confident. Physical stress is reduced and vitality is increased.[18]

To summarize, in your Next House do you want to be healthier? Would you like to have less stress, less sense of hurt, and less anger? Would you like to be able to forgive more quickly when other bad stuff enters your life? In your Next House, would you like to be more compassionate, self-confident, and relaxed? Will you want to experience a sense of vitality? All that is there for your taking simply through the act of forgiving.

We needn't look for research to convince us that lack of forgiveness impacts our relationships. Who wants to be around a negative person who is constantly living in their victimhood? Anger, even when we think we've pushed it below the surface, shows itself in irritability and that mood of "might explode at any time." We all prefer to move away from that person. Those folks don't even need to speak one word. Their countenance warns us to stay out of their space.

> Jesus never asks us to do something He Himself did not do.

Better physical health in our Now House may even speed our move into our Next House as energy is no longer spent on anger, resentment, and defending our victimhood. That energy can be invested making those necessary changes in our new life.

Physical health is a good thing. Spiritual health is even better. And forgiveness is key. Let's look at the spiritual aspects of forgiveness.

While most religions include forgiveness as an important part of spiritual life, Christianity makes forgiveness a benchmark of behavior. In the Sermon on the Mount, Jesus repeatedly spoke of this. Jesus taught, "Blessed are the merciful, for they will be shown mercy" (Matthew 5:7). Do we wish for others and God to show us mercy while we're in our Now House? Of course! The prerequisite is that we need to show mercy to others. (Yes, to *all* others.)

Jesus also said, "And when you stand praying, if you hold anything against anyone, forgive them, so that your Father in heaven may forgive you your sins" (Mark 11:25). Are we prone to wrong behavior, regardless of our circumstances and which House we're in at the time? Of course! Do we want and need forgiveness? Of course! We want and need

God to "forgive us our trespasses" (Matthew 6:15 NKJV).

Has someone wronged us? We believe so. As we are praying, does that grudge nudge us? Our humanoid heart wants to ask God to get even, get back for us what they took and more. But clearly God says, "Forgive them." We need to forgive them even before asking God for forgiveness for ourselves.

The forgiveness Jesus taught goes beyond what we can accomplish on our own: "But to you who are listening I say: Love your enemies, do good to those who hate you, bless those who curse you, pray for those who mistreat you. If someone slaps you on one cheek, turn to them the other also. If someone takes your coat, do not withhold your shirt from them" (Luke 6:27–29). This sounds extreme, and indeed it is. That's why for some of us it is impossible in our humanness. Yes, we can forgive the small stuff on our own, but not the biggies. Let's talk about how we can manage that impossible task of forgiveness in His strength, not our own.

Jesus never asks us to do something He Himself did not do. He was murdered. In His last breaths before death, He asked His Father to forgive those who were murdering Him. That's extreme. He prayed, "Father, forgive them, for they do not know what they are doing" (Luke 23:34). And the soldiers divided up His clothes by casting lots.

We protest. Those men *did* know what they were doing. They beat Him, pounded the nails, hoisted the cross. They were intentional, not oblivious; there was no accident here! So why does Jesus say they didn't know what they were doing? Because what they did not know, nor understand, was the eternal consequence of their wrongdoing. Some were carrying out orders. Some were killing their competition. Some were trying to protect their superior spiritual standing—as they saw it. They each had their reasons for participating in His murder, and they thought they had succeeded.

What these people did not know was that they were destroying themselves by the evil they were succeeding in accomplishing. They were oblivious to the fact that their own hearts would be poisoned by the evil they were doing. Their perspectives on everything, every day, from that day forward would be tainted at least by the necessity of justifying, excusing, and defending their action on the day of Christ's death. Worse, they would need to take more evil action to support this great evil they had already done or to cover it up. That included bribing people to lie and more. The leaders who ordered Christ's death thought they were taking care of business. In fact, they were not only revealing their own character, they were destroying it.

And even worse, these misguided individuals had rejected the only person who could have given them a future in the perfect Final House. They didn't get it. But someday they will understand. They will recognize what they refused to recognize at that time.

Those who have hurt you, who have caused your loss—even if they are willfully intentional in what they are doing and do succeed in taking something precious from you—have hurt themselves deeply in the long term. If they never need to face that reality in their lifetime, that moment will come. We know that often justice does not roll down here on earth. But this life on this earth is not the final chapter. Our moving into our Next House, which might appear to others to be misshapen, less than it could be because of our loss, is not our Final House. And that's the House that counts.

When seen through the lens of Jesus' experience and what we learn from it, those who intentionally contributed to our loss, deserve our pity. It may take awhile for us to wrap our minds around that reality and for our feelings to fall in line, but it is possible. If we see our offenders as Jesus saw His murderers, we can forgive as He did, on His strength and example, not our own.

Forgiving other people is not easy, free, or cheap. When we forgive, we pay a price and become willing ourselves to bear the pain of our loss. That hurt is real, possibly or probably justified, and can't be denied, swept under the rug, or pretended out of existence. We agree in our hearts and minds to carry that pain and roll it over onto Jesus' strong shoulders so we can move on in freedom into our Next House.

We will have more than one "mountain of forgiveness" to climb, beyond those who are responsible for the significant loss we have suffered. But a new habit is being developed. Forgiveness in the future will come easier and in a more broad range of circumstances. That's good news.

With time and thought, we ultimately face the reality that God allowed our loss. So we must face Him as well. I discovered with every loss in my life that God welcomed my "Why?" as well as any other question. He was not put off by my anger, but rather He tenderly taught me where that anger needed to be directed.

How could God allow good people to suffer? How could God allow good people to die? Isn't our anger at Him justified? His power can cause or prevent all things. Right? I wrestled with these truths and was angry at God when my husband died. In my book for widows, I wrote about how I just didn't happen to be one of those people who have never questioned God, those who have the simple faith to accept whatever comes their way.[19] God never turned away from me or said, "Talk to the hand." He simply taught me, welcomed me into a graduate class on forgiveness.

A simple, yet profound truth is that illness, death, pain, and destruction were not God's plan but the result of us humanoids taking matters into our own hands. He has chosen not to intervene yet, though He must be saddened and angry at all the messes here on this planet. He still grants freedom on this earth. When He makes his final intervention, our Final House will have none of this bad stuff. That's the big picture. But we're not there yet.

In the case of my own losses, God was never stumped or surprised by my senseless rantings and ravings. He reminded me of an earlier time and lessons I learned when I was required to forgive as I never had before. A person I treasured was snared in a legal nightmare. Brazenly one lawyer and one judge took his freedom, his future, his youth, and his trust. I tried to make sense of injustice in a system that was supposed to deliver justice. God did not reveal any ray of light, comfort, or fairness that would ever happen to those individuals who looked on at us in those courtrooms with disdain and superiority. Rather, God let me glimpse heaven, where His ways will rule and everything will be just.

God never stopped reaching out to me, though I deserved a time-out for my immature conclusions about what God should be up to in this universe, based on my desires and perspectives rather than on His all-knowing, all-loving perspective.

In short, God consistently loved and embraced me through all my struggle. Through that experience, I discovered that God did not need my forgiveness. In fact, I no longer felt that He was anyone or anything but good. It was this messed-up world and its systems and other humanoids that needed my forgiveness.

Settling things with God is better done sooner than later. He's waiting for you, and will stay with you through the questions and confusion as long as it takes. You'll be amazed at the incredible sense of relief and peace when you settle it all with God.

Are we done forgiving yet? Possibly not. There's that face staring back from the mirror. Sometimes it is ourselves we need to forgive.

Anyone who claims to have no regrets about anything in the past is probably delusional, in denial, or both. Our best efforts on our good days are imperfect. The reality is that forgiving ourselves is the most important of all acts of forgiveness. Others we need to forgive are out there at different places, distances, and spaces in our lives. But we live in our own skin 24–7, all the time, every day. Forgiving ourselves is vital.

Perhaps you need to forgive yourself for a behavior that still threatens to become a part of your life again. If that's the case, waste no time in surrounding yourself with strong accountability partners and avoiding every area of temptation. Run—don't walk!—or that habit will be stale air, old furniture, polluted water in your Next House.

Forgiving ourselves is essential for our future. If we forgive all others and not ourselves, the difference of all those other acts of forgiveness is minuscule compared to continuing to carry our guilt.

Question: How great was our wrong?

Answer: How great is Jesus' capacity to shoulder our wrong and forgive us? Gargantuous. Remember, He forgave His murderers. He can and will forgive us.

MAKING AMENDS, MENDING RELATIONSHIPS

Related to this important topic of forgiveness is that of making amends and mending relationships when things have gone wrong.

We may wish we were capable of making full restoration to those we have wronged in the past. Probably it can't be done, although repaying what we can repay is important. Beyond that, we can pray that God restore to them what we are not able to restore.

Mending relationships can get complicated—since it has to do with people. While mending relationships is desirable, it is not always possible. Romans 12:18 reminds us, "If it is possible, as far as it depends on you, live at peace with everyone." Things happen in relationships that should not happen. One person may be willing to build back the bridge of relationship, but that bridge can't be built if the offense is ongoing. It takes two to create peace.

That first step of attempting to reconcile the relationship is not easy. If it were, our Creator wouldn't have found it necessary to outline for us exactly what we need to do. Why does Scripture give us specific steps for resolving conflict? Because we humans can easily take a bad situation and make it worse. We can stuff the problem away, fearful of talking to the person, but our annoyance will likely show itself sometime, somewhere. We can take the bull-in-the-china-shop approach and attack. We can approach that other person with our own agenda—hoping to make ourselves look good or look strong, unwilling to consider a viewpoint other than our own. None of these approaches are God-honoring. Both feed the beast stalking within us, our human nature to defend ourselves, to make ourselves look good.

Scripture directs us first to talk with the person (Matthew 18:15). Seek understanding. That step alone is humbling. We may learn a perspective that surprises us. That step requires that we listen. We also take note of whether that other person is listening to us as well.

What signals that listening is happening? The best clue is that questions are being asked, with the mutual give-and-take of both parties, when one is not monopolizing the conversation. Resolution may come. There might be those Ah-ha moments when one says, "I didn't realize that's how you heard what I was saying," "I didn't know that was so important to you," "What I meant was . . . ," and "I didn't realize your priorities." Clear communication is vital in this step.

If the two of you speak and cannot come to resolution, bring in another person (Matthew 18:16). This is humbling as well, as our own motives are on display. That other person needs to be a respected person who can bring objectivity to the table, not only to hear both sides, but to hold up the mirror of reality to both parties. If an attempt at two-way communication has not brought understanding, that third party can see and bring a perspective that perhaps neither could see on his or her own.

God has a plan beyond just reconciliation in these circumstances. Conflict is an opportunity for each of us to see our own flaws and weaknesses. He wants humble followers, not self-righteous, prideful folks. Solving conflict God's way produces humility. We see things in ourselves that need to change. We learn to be clearer in our communication. We often learn as well that fewer words are better than more. There is much that truly is better left unsaid. Before you speak, consider: Does what you want to say build up? bring healing? promote peace?

Usually at some point while we're in the process of trying to reconcile with another person, we want to throw our hands up and back out. Why? Because most of us do not like conflict, and it's hard work that consumes much energy. Recently I was in a reconciliation process when I had loads of other things to do that were more fun and seemed to me more rewarding. But backing out seemed like the better option only at the moment. If I had quit at that point, it would have closed the door to all I could learn and the others involved as well. I'd have lost the freedom of letting go. In my specific situation, I needed to grow in my leadership role and skills. Staying in that process was not only a requirement, it was the right thing to do.

If we back out when the reconciling process gets tough, we will probably also back away in future situations. Families, friends, at work, in churches—conflict happens everywhere. Our choice to avoid it is simply not good for our future and will mean that our Next House will not be all that it can be.

Ever practical and addressing every humanoid issue, Scripture continues with the specific how-tos in Matthew 18:15–17. The first step was conversing, with good listening, one-on-one with the other person. If understanding at that point did not happen, we took the second step and brought in another person. If that wise person's objectivity and help to navigate the relationship to bring reconciliation was not successful, Scripture recommends distancing ourselves from that person.

Those words sound simple. The required actions for attempting reconciliation are difficult and sometimes even extremely painful, at least in the short term. Those simple-sounding steps, in fact, require lots of courage—and always lots of prayer. And then, if reconciliation is impossible, we need to learn to move on given that reality.

What does a good "Move On" look like? It is characterized two ways: definite and kind.

DEFINITE

Dr. Henry Cloud explains this clearly in his book *Necessary Endings*. As it relates to being definite, he states, "Above all, don't be squishy."[20]

Leaving loose ends or putting a clear break off, saying "maybe next time" is the same as deciding that you are willing to go through the conflict again with the same results. What's good about that? Nothing.

Often we are indefinite because we so wish to be understood. We want to be seen as that nice person who always leaves the door open. But think of our room analogy again. We want to move from our Now House to our Next House. Leaving an open door with that person of conflict means the chaos will follow you into your Next House. Do you want that? If you have gone through this process and the other party does not understand you and will not be reconciled to you, the reconciliation won't happen. Give up that wish.

We may not wish to declare a definite ending because we feel it's a failure in some way and exiting means it's over. True. But that ending is necessary. Staying in the conflict does not equate success.

KIND

When conflict cannot be resolved, we can be tempted to be unkind. A good "Move On" is kind. The benefits are many.

When we keep our interaction kind, we reinforce our own character as being kind and we'll be stronger in the future for it. We're behaving to match the fact that we've forgiven, whether or not the other party asked for the forgiveness. Forgiving will lessen our pain after our exit. Even after necessary endings, there may be some things we miss, and that void is painful.

We don't know the future. That person may appear in our life again for some reason we would not imagine today. That event will be better if we have ended this relationship in a kind way.

Think of that other person for a moment. That person needs to move on as well. How will your kindness impact them? Let's take the naysayer's approach first. What if we end with harsh, angry words at them? That lends credibility to their tendency to feel, "Just as I thought. Not a nice person. The proof is in the pudding." But what if you are kind in that ending? That person will see you moving on in freedom and more contentment. They reflect on their behavior in comparison.

I've been walking with a wise friend lately. We shared some of our struggles in our leadership roles. We've both been in positions where we needed to address behavior that needed to be changed. We were in that conflict resolution role. And when change did not happen, we were the ones who had to deliver the bad news. Who wants to be the one to hear that!? Truth-telling was required, and our positions of leadership meant that we had to be the truth teller. A business connection was over, and not all parties would be happy with that outcome. She reminded me that truth must be accompanied with empathy.

Truth plus empathy immediately gives any leader a servant-hearted, love-covered voice. How many times has God gently corrected me, given me another chance, loved me with a tenderness I did not deserve?

For those of us who dislike conflict—which may be a part of the truth-telling process—empathy is oil on the waters. Truth plus empathy—that's how Jesus led. Truth defines the facts. Empathy soothes the feelings.

In my new role as a ministry leader, I'm expected to steer the ship. In my case this small business is a not-for-profit with a clear mission statement to guide us in what we do and what we don't do. You may be that leader in a large company, a ministry, a village, city, state, or nation. Wisdom is our greatest need. But wisdom without being willing to tell the truth can be weakness. Isaiah was a prophet, a leader. God showed him the truth. Read Isaiah 6. God needed a spokesperson. Isaiah responded, "Here I am. Send me!"

And then God showed him how REALLY hard the job would be. He had an incredibly difficult message to deliver. His reward? Chapter 66:2 tells us that God looked on him with favor because he was humble, contrite, and reverent of God's words.

In those places where our task is hard and conflict possible, maybe even probable, we need a clear sense of who we are and a clear idea of the outcome we wish. Knowing who we are gives us courage to stay in the process until it is resolved. Knowing the desired outcome, we have a clear recognition of when to move on.

Our prayer can be for courage to tell the truth, clarity that we be accurately heard, and empathy that we be kind. Be ready to forgive and love. That's what Jesus would do.

A FRESH START IN THE NEXT HOUSE

Let's look at some of the differences forgiveness will make in our Next House.

If you have gone through the conflict resolution process as outlined in Matthew and needed to move on because resolution was impossible, you have become a wiser person. You take this wisdom into your Next House. It is likely that you will, in your Next House, be a better discerner of people than you were in the past. We talked about fools in chapter four. Having gone through the process of forgiving, you see more clearly that person whose behavior shows you the stuff they are made of.

You will more readily recognize that someone might be a good friend—for someone else. Or you'll realize more rapidly that someone might be a person to date with a view to a long-term relationship—for someone else. You'll discern when another person might be a good employer or employee—for someone else. We know ourselves better, and see more clearly those with whom we will be compatible in relationships, in a work environment, in volunteer positions.

In our Next House, we will likely pause longer, listen more carefully, and speak fewer, more carefully chosen words because of what we learned in our past experiences in forgiveness.

In our Next House, we'll probably avoid some situations we might have embraced before. We'll read the fine print more carefully, sign on the dotted line more slowly, not join in a partnership or contractual agreement so readily.

And what has motivated us to become wiser? We have learned that things can go south, or terribly wrong, and cannot always be remedied or restored.

In our Next House, we will also be more likely to document, document, document. This might be in keeping records as it relates to a business venture or insurance claim. What is happening? Is this a person of their word? Are they consistent? What can I count on?

In a personal relationship, that documentation might be in a journal or diary, as we take more serious notice of behaviors. Words said. Words kept? Words not kept. Loan made? Loan repaid. Loan not repaid. Co-signed agreement? Agreement honored. Agreement ignored.

Fool me once—you're the fool. Fool me twice—I'm the fool. We learn.

In our Next House we recognize that forgiveness is costly. We decided back in our Now House to absorb the loss, accepting the pain of that loss in order to forgive. We have decided not to continue to be abused or taken advantage of. We've appropriately closed that door and lived that necessary ending. In our Next House we need to be cautious not to fill that void with an impulsive, I-need-to-feel-better-at-the-moment action.

Since we are creatures of habit we might be tempted to shape the Next House like the Before House, returning to an old, ineffective way of dealing with voids in our life. We might want to hoard, hand out, hunger, hide, or hibernate. These did not help us before. We have better options in our new life. I understand the temptation to fill that void quickly without considering the consequences. We might want to fill that void with something entirely different in order to experience the rush of entering an unknown.

Necessary endings are new opportunities that should be entered with care, common sense, and clear thinking. Here's how not to do it.

When I was in my Now House after becoming single again, I wanted something so demanding and different that I would be excited to hear the alarm in the morning. I wanted to feel invigorated and challenged at the beginning of each new day. So I decided I'd become a Rehab Queen. I planned to buy battered houses, fix them up, sell them at a profit, and move on to the next project. I'd buy overalls so I could have that square pencil in one front pocket, my measuring device in another. I might even hang a hammer in that side loop. Of course, I'd have my ever-ready traveling coffee mug with flavored hot gourmet coffee. And I might even need a pickup truck. I started taking classes in real estate. Fun.

I tromped through foreclosed disasters with staircases ripped out, rust-encrusted toilet bowls, and water-damaged walls. I entered a crowded, standing-room-only event in the downtown room of bidders on Chicago properties. One needs lots of cash (I mean thousands) in your pocket before you raise your hand in the bid. Strangely, I was the only woman there. Also, I was truly not dressed for this crowd. Nothing in my wardrobe was strange enough to fit in. Yes, I was stared at! However, I was confident. This was my new life, and I had done my homework on the properties being offered that day. I was experiencing the rush of entering the unknown.

What I had not done was mentally review my credentials to be the Rehab Queen: A master's degree in counseling, twenty-three years' experience counseling teens, three years teaching psychology in high schools, three years teaching psychology in a university, writing ten books, international travel. Oh, and, two years of successfully appealing my property taxes.

I had never bid on property at an auction, painted a room, or created an extensive contract with a construction contractor. I had never supervised a construction crew, selected multiple appliances, or applied for permits in city and village halls. But there was that void moving from my

Now House to my Next House that needed to be filled!

I did my homework on three properties and took it all the way to the bidding phases for these distressed homes. I knew my rehab costs and figured my top dollar to bid. I could envision myself in that pickup with Rehab Queen painted in pink and red letters on the doors and across the back window.

I lost all three to a higher bidder. That was early in 2007—just before the recession hit with its heavy blows to real estate and building construction.

Thank God! I lost! I would have been mid-mess in the middle of the market meltdown, a Rehab Slave rather than Queen.

Why tell you this goofy but true story? So you think more carefully than I did. OK, at least, I did not get caught up in the bidding frenzy and go over my absolute top number. I treasured once again those words in Psalm 116:6: "The Lord preserves the simple" (NKJV).

Moving from the Now House to our Next House is likely to happen in fits and starts with lots of parts in motion. We need every ounce of wisdom and careful thought we can muster plus our Board of Directors and forgiveness homework as nearly completed as possible. That does not guarantee a fabulous Next House. But a stronger, healthier Next House is more likely.

How important is forgiving to your future? I'd like to share an example from one of my experiences as a counselor and educator. In the large public high school, my job as a counselor included academic monitoring of students assigned to me. I identified a group of students who had multiple failing grades in their first quarter. They had several common characteristics. I decided I needed to get to know them better in order to determine effective interventions.

We formed a group, they told me their names, and we began to meet regularly. By happenstance they were all girls. They were hesitant to say much, though there were only six and they knew each other from their neighborhood. I decided to introduce a cut-and-paste project to stimulate discussion.

I brought six poster boards, stacks of magazines, scissors, and paste to the next meeting. I asked them first to take their poster board and fold it into thirds. At the top of the left third they wrote *Today*. At the top of the right third they wrote *Future*. In the middle section they wrote *From Here to There*. I ask them to draw or find pictures that represented their lives today and do the same for each section. What did they want their future to look like? What were their plans to get from today to the future they desired?

Our meetings took on a new energy. They chattered as they cut, pasted, and wrote. I listened and watched. The *Today* section filled up quickly with pictures of pizza, boys, pretty clothes, and titles of songs. The *Future* section began to be filled with pictures of pretty houses, often a professional career picture, sometimes pictures of children and vacation destinations.

But the *From Here to There* section remained blank. Noticing that, I initiated what became an interesting discussion: How do you get from where you are now to where you want to be?

The girls simply did not know. That became the foundation for my intervention plans. We planned events to address this blank space. I invited professional women of their cultural background to come to our school and make presentations about their careers and educational paths. The girls identified friends they thought would benefit from some events provided by the group. I expanded the invitation list to other students I identified. I began to take them on college campus tours.

The young women were required to make up classwork and homework they missed by attending an event. We always had good snacks. Five years later the group had expanded to a school service club. But my greatest satisfaction was that all but one of them earned her high school diploma.

So how does this relate to our forgiveness topic? Might I suggest that you take a piece of paper, fold it in thirds, and complete a similar exercise? Above the left third write *Before House*, above the right third write *Next House*, and above the middle third write *Now House*. Whether you write, list, or draw pictures, fill in those spaces with what was or is or you wish to be in each section.

In your Before House section you might describe or illustrate what was important to you in the past. Include the event and people involved in your loss.

I imagine in your Next House space you might list health, spiritual wholeness, satisfying relationships, vigor, happiness, and peace. You might also have listed building a legacy that's good for those who come after you. Satisfying work and the opportunity to serve others might also appear in that space.

Take a bold marker and in that Now House space write *forgive.* That costly, difficult action is the most important one you'll take to make your Next House the best that it can be.

6

The Party You (Didn't Know You) Wanted

I hope you see now that my words in the introduction were not a feel-good theory, but a realistic option for you regardless of your loss. I've shared my story from my chaotic first trip to Africa, which had every appearance of a crash and burn effort, to leaping off a cliff for the sheer beauty of the experience. I hope after laughing both at me and with me, you can glimpse a party ahead for you. Now turn to the mirror and determine that the smile will be for you.

I share the losses I've lived so that you can see that we ordinary humanoids are capable of productive and positive lives in our Next House. My promise to you is based on seeing the nature of our human spirits. We yearn not just to discover new meaning in our new circumstances, but to live it. Good things can be yours. My friend Lori, who became a single mom at age thirty-eight, was challenged to mow her own yard, be involved in her son's sports teams, and discover who she was apart from the man she had married at age nineteen. Mother/daughter things came a bit easier. Tea at the American Girl store was more her comfort zone than finding football cleats. She said to me with quiet strength, "I'm going to choose to live well."

With that attitude, Lori embraces today. One of her recent adventures was going to dinner in a quaint and charming lakeside town, on the back of a motorcycle! Yes, there is a new friend in her life. "It was scary at first, but then quite fun and exciting," were her words. She is living well indeed!

Having heard the stories I've shared and the hearts of courage each represents, I'm trusting that by now you have decided that you will not keep your kaleidoscope pointed toward the black hole of your loss. How others see you in your loss is not what counts. It's what you determine to do with that loss that matters. You have been changed by that loss, but not defined by it.

Of course, you cannot return to the life you had before your loss. We recognized in chapter two that we can't have *IT* back. I hope that you've been able not just to relax that grip on your past, but to open your palms completely and let go of your expectations and dreams based on that past. The road forward is neither smooth nor easy. But it's time to tilt your kaleidoscope toward the light and see what beauty and intricate new combinations emerge.

Maybe the void that was screaming to be filled has already taken on a new melody. I hope so! That's the sound of opportunity. And opportunity is the birthplace of innovation. I call that place of innovation the party you (didn't know you) wanted.

Let's look at what you take to the party.

NEW STRENGTH

The problem you faced changed you. Did you feel weak, defeated, and vulnerable during and coming out of that loss? Probably. But that struggle has made you stronger. You typically don't discover that strength you have gained until it becomes necessary for a new event or opportunity. That strength is dormant until you take action where that strength is required.

I thought after my husband's wicked terminal disease, I would return to being the person I was before. I had grown up in a culture where little girls were polite and it was important to "make nice." We were taught that it was better to keep people smiling than disagree or say no. That perspective impacted my behavior through my adult years. And often it was good.

However, during my husband's disease, I had to be a tough advocate with insurance companies, assistive device providers, and long-term health care organizations, to mention a few. I became the queen of "I won't take no for an answer."

"I've read the fine print here, and this is what you *will* do."

"Yes, that battery is one half the cost, but it won't provide the options for a two-hundred-pound man, and it's not what the prescription says." (And I love that man—that's why I'll be all over this until you say yes!)

"Please transfer me to your legal department."

While I was dealing with illness (a wicked disease, to be sure), becoming a tough advocate, and struggling with anticipatory grief, a woman I never knew existed was emerging.

I sat with our clinic's social worker warming my cold fingers around my favorite coffee: skim cappuccino. The Chicago cold outside was warmer than the ice in my soul. Even Caribou Coffee's cheerful fire could not warm me.

"Will I be nice again when this is over?" I asked.

"No, you won't," was her answer. "You'll never be the same."

She was right, and for good reason. That season of loss required that I grow in assertiveness. It required me to study fine print and to document, document, document. It required me to keep organized records. And it required me to learn terminology unknown to me before. These were necessary in my season of loss.

Furthermore, God had an assignment ahead that required that I be experienced in all those assets that I had never needed before.

It has been said that the hottest fires make the hardest steel. I needed that hot fire to equip me. That will likely be true for you too.

If your loss has been due to divorce, you too have learned more about legal obligations than you knew before. You've probably learned more about finances, bank accounts, and maybe even prenuptial agreements than you ever envisioned.

If your loss has been due to bankruptcy or foreclosure, you know more about mortgages, equity, and terms like *under water* that have meanings you did not think about before.

How would you describe this season of loss? Stress-filled? A time for swapping delusions for reality? A time for de-cluttering your life to simply accomplish the necessary?

There's another word that now describes you because of this season: strong.

SIMPLE AND SATISFIED

Loss has a way of refining not just us but our lifestyles and living spaces. Even if our loss is something taken that we did not wish to give up, we have been forced to learn to live without it. Embracing our Big Blue Bowl perspective, we recognize that some of what we can no longer have is really not such a big deal after all.

It's easier to find things in a mostly empty refrigerator.

Decision time in deciding what to wear is quick and easy when the closet is small and the choices are few.

Smaller living spaces mean less time and money for upkeep.

Selecting a vacation spot is simple when there's no money for travel. A stay-cation, with picnics in the local park, will do.

Emotional energy for self-care is available after exercising necessary endings in some relationships.

Time for exercise and even quiet times of reflection are real benefits of our new life with less.

Wandering time in the tool and home improvement stores or shopping malls is past. We now have time to volunteer to help someone else in a tight spot.

We begin to like what's in our Big Blue Bowl. We begin to notice and examine verses in Scripture we breezed past before, like Psalm 116:6–7, which says to God, "You protect ordinary people, and when I was helpless, You saved me and treated me so kindly that I don't need to worry anymore" (my paraphrase).

We look at our budget from before our loss and see the amounts we spent on needs and wants, and now we realize that lots of those needs were a mirage. We don't really need that particular living space. Some have found they don't need a car. Our neighborhood knows that at 7:14 a.m. a lawyer pedals by, biking to the train station. A car to him is a "want," not a "need."

How many of us would never have looked from the mesmerizing mirage of what we thought were needs and wants without our season of loss? And how many of us could have imagined we would sense such profound satisfaction at living with less? I, for one, raise my hand.

Less stuff means less upkeep on stuff. That equates to less stress, more time, and more of ourselves to invest in what matters to us now.

My trips to Africa, with their purpose of visiting and empowering widows, highlighted for me the blessing of my new, simple life.

I entered the six-by-nine-foot living room/kitchen of a widow in the Mathare Valley slums of Nairobi. A drape hung to cover a four-by-nine-foot area for sleeping. Six people live in this space. They have one meal a day, and that may be only rice. Meat and vegetables are rare in their home. The widowed mother, Beatrice, has a quiet and almost content smile. All eyes around her, teens and little children have a haunting hungry look. They depend on her. I recognize the extreme blessing and wealth of the life I'm now living. Returning to my routine in my own home, I enjoy healthy toast and flavored coffee to start my day, followed by at least another meal that might be only protein and vegetables—rare miraculous treats to that widow's family.

Traveling to Africa, which always paints my life-party with vibrant new colors, might not be an option for you to help you see colors in your kaleidoscope in a new light. But volunteer to serve breakfast at a PADS location near you or at the local Salvation Army shelter. Volunteer to be the delivery driver for Meals on Wheels or other community services to the needy or homeless. You'll find yourself looking in the mirror and with a nod and a smile, quietly affirming that the simplicity of your life is satisfying.

SINGLE OR MARRIED—AND SATISFIED

If your loss means that you are single again, moments will come when you consider, "Is this the life I want?" That's a big and important question.

Regardless of whether you answer yes or no, the follow-up is complicated. If we choose to be single, what and how we deal with solitude and loneliness are important. If we want another person in our life, how we navigate new relationships will be equally important.

How we hunger for connection! While many of us intend to remain single and become comfortable with our new life alone, many do not. Statistics tell us that half of all marriages end in divorce. That's not very encouraging. Statistics also tell us that second marriages are more at risk, with a 75 percent likelihood of ending in divorce.

If you are divorced and want to remarry, I'd encourage you to read Dr. Henry Cloud's excellent book *Necessary Endings*, which I've referenced before.[21] While much of the book's content refers to necessary endings in business settings, it contains much wisdom about considering personal habits and qualities. Discovering the patterns that contributed to a divorce and addressing those enhances the likelihood of a subsequent marriage being a success.

Statistics tell us that more widowers remarry than widows. Since the average age of widows is in the mid-fifties, it's not surprising that looking for a new companion is likely and appropriate. But many who might wish to remarry do not find a suitable match.

One widow wrote Widowconnection.com, telling about how God was satisfying her needs in so many ways. And yet she added, "So I have the love I have always wanted. But some real arms would be OK." We can relate!

Another widow told of her hasty marriage to a widower and their divorce only a few years later. Her conclusion was that they married too soon without considering the difficulties ahead.

One woman wrote wondering whether the fact that she was nearly the same age of her widower friend's daughter would be a problem. My answer? Probably, at some point. The same would be true for divorced persons marrying. Age and children's ages are factors.

A new relationship is not to be lightly undertaken. Remember that we are vulnerable in our grief. Wisdom may get buried under impulse, especially if we are struggling to get a handle on our new lives. Another relationship to solve a problem—like loneliness, financial difficulties, or home repairs—rarely solves the problem and usually brings new problems we did not have before!

So, keeping it real and brief, here are a few guidelines:

Always, always connect only when you are both like-minded in your faith.

Don't hurry, please. The guideline of "no major decision for two years" is a good one.

Children will be a factor. Whether young or old, your children's parent whether dad or mom will always be important, and carry influence. They will have myriad feelings attached to seeing you with someone else. Whether they've lost a parent due to divorce or death, younger children seem to adjust more quickly in that new marriage.

Ask the opinion of others you trust, and listen to them carefully. They often have better relational eyesight into others than we have at the moment.

Study the Scriptures on remarriage. Your prayers over the open Bible will invite God's special wisdom and protection into your life.

Proceed with caution, prayer, joy, and anticipation. A great future is not dependent on a new person in your life, but on your connection with your Creator.

An important question to ask yourself before getting involved in a new relationship is this: Am I whole? In other words, have I grieved and healed from my loss? Can I live on my own? Am I self-sufficient with finances and work? No human being can fill all the voids in your life. Expecting that is asking for disaster.

Deciding to be single has its challenges and rewards. What will you do when those empty hours seem to yawn before you? It's good to have a plan. A few good novels on a nightstand might be the answer at one time. Friends you can call or connect with are also a good option. What movies might you enjoy together? One single-again woman made it her goal to do one thing a month she had never done before. She kept to her plan for one year—as long as it was necessary. She camped, planted a tree, learned to dance, and undertook other adventures. New and deeper friendships grew from those shared experiences and helped her move forward in her new life as a single person.

Yes, it takes time to discover what you love to do with your solitude. For many of us, we learn to love it, and miss those hours if our lives get too packed and time alone is crowded out.

Eating what we want on a random schedule, not dealing with someone else's clutter, freedom to travel based only on our calendar, our list of freedoms is as long as we wish. Exercising those freedoms builds a sense of contentment we never knew would be possible in our season of loss.

It is now, after all, our party.

Before we leave the topic of satisfaction in our new life, I'd like to point out why it's so difficult in our culture for us to embrace satisfaction with a new life that may not look like the dream life, or even normal life in our culture. In 1943, psychologist Abraham Maslow proposed a hierarchy of needs that supposedly described the stages of growth in humans. His

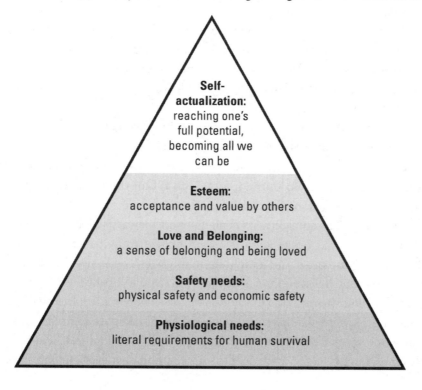

Self-actualization: reaching one's full potential, becoming all we can be

Esteem: acceptance and value by others

Love and Belonging: a sense of belonging and being loved

Safety needs: physical safety and economic safety

Physiological needs: literal requirements for human survival pyramid assumes that needs at the bottom of the pyramid must be satisfied before the most desirable goals at the top become a reality.[22]

More description of these needs appear in the study guide. This theory became so popular that it has influenced most of contemporary opinions about the basic necessities of a satisfied life.

Loss typically shakes or even removes the middle of the pyramid—love and belonging. The group with whom we identified and socialized with before may be drastically changed by our experience of loss. And it may be that the one we loved and who loved us most is the one we've lost. That reality rearranges the top two sections of the pyramid as well. No wonder it's so hard for us to move forward. Maslow's theory is the basis for psychological perspectives in traditional texts and is the basis for advertising and a host of other influences that bombard each of us daily.

Recognizing the strong influence of this theory helps us resist that false assumption of what is necessary for satisfaction in our lives.

Depending on our loss, our sense of belonging may never be achieved by the yardstick of our popular culture. We may be invisible in many circumstances and marginalized in others. Physical love and intimacy may never again be a part of our lives. If Maslow is right, we will never be able to hold ourselves in the esteem that is healthy in our new lives. If he's right, a satisfying life achieving esteem and self-actualization is impossible. No new party for us.

Why is his theory wrong? He leaves out the element of God, His creation of us, and the satisfaction we sense in fulfilling His purposes. That theory leaves out the beyond-human sense of belonging when we identify with our Creator. It leaves out the satisfaction of giving up physical intimacy for a love and intimacy that's greater than human sexuality.

Celibacy in our culture is considered a state of denial and minimized living rather than a positive choice to focus on other passions—a choice that Jesus, the apostle Paul, the prophetess Anna, and millions of others have made through the ages.

We've referred earlier to the words Paul wrote to us in Romans 12:2: "Do not conform to the pattern of this world, but be transformed by the renewing of your mind. Then you will be able to test and approve what

God's will is—his good, pleasing and perfect will."

Conforming to cultural expectations is one option we have. This will likely leave us feeling shortchanged and "not meeting expectations." Or we can be transformed and let our minds expand to a bigger view of our new world. In it we can test out our new options for living. We test and approve our new party with its unexpected satisfactions. And more important than our personal approval of our new party, is His. Esteem and self-actualization of a more important kind are ours.

KINGDOM EQUITY

So now you've arrived at your new party. You are strong, simple, single or married, and satisfied. What's next?

Let me introduce you to a new concept: Kingdom Equity.

A stranger approached me after I'd made a presentation to a hospital staff in Lilongwe, Malawi. "Miriam Neff," he declared, "you are rich in Kingdom Equity."

I was more than puzzled; I was intrigued.

I asked if we could talk a bit more after I'd greeted the departing staff. We did. We found a quiet corner where he introduced himself and explained what had brought him to Africa. He already had heard my story and knew why I was there.

Having never heard of Kingdom Equity before, I asked him to explain the concept. He explained Kingdom Equity as God's investment in you. Our Creator, God, is building a good place for us. Yes, Kingdom Equity is about heaven, but it also refers to good places and good things here on this earth. God not only desires our best in this Kingdom, He wants us to contribute to this Kingdom on earth being better for others.

Here's the definition: Kingdom Equity is God's investment in you. Events, whether positive or negative, *gift* you with wisdom, experience, information, and faith. Everything in your life is a part of God building equity (valuable investment) into your life.

I certainly understood the concept of equity as it relates to finances. We have all had wake-up calls recently. We understand that equity in our home is value. Equity in investments is the worth of that purse. Equity is a good thing to have.

This new acquaintance began to describe what he saw as God's equity building in my life.

A farm girl learning to sew on a treadle Singer sewing machine.

(God knew I'd need that later.)

A farm girl living temporarily in a home with no indoor plumbing.

(Also needed in Africa.)

World travels that left me hungry for more planet-roaming experiences.

A courageous attitude, "Let's get at it" spirit. Or, as my husband described it, my absence of a fear chip factor.

He continued the list from the little he knew of me in that one meeting.

I rapidly took notes, recognizing that I wanted to add to his list. This new perspective cast a different and valuable light on seemingly ordinary qualities and experiences, and even hardships. I began to see things in my past that had current Kingdom Equity value.

Kingdom Equity was a precious concept that pieced together what I had often seen as random events in my past. But they were not random. God was investing in me intentionally. He was building Kingdom Equity.

Seemingly throwaway skills were on the list that included important earned degrees. A home destroyed by fire added Kingdom Equity to my life.

I have no idea how long that conversation lasted. It seemed too brief. We both had to move on to our next commitments.

Under my mosquito net that night with a feeble bedside lamp, I was grateful that the sporadic electricity stayed on. I scribbled as long as my tired body would allow. I looked again at my scribbled notes from our conversation. My final entry quoting his words read: "You've got it, Miriam. Now spend it."

SPENDING YOUR KINGDOM EQUITY

Before you embark on your spending spree, let's review.

You Won't Spend It If . . .

You won't spend it if . . . you're stuck thinking the future must look like the past. Remember chapter one.

Here's a test question on that. What is the news in your life today? Is today's reality what you would have predicted one year ago? Probably not. I would have not predicted the stock market's volatility. Swings of four hundred points are now common. Most of us would have predicted that housing prices would have rebounded—at least a bit. Our neighborhood values are still down 40 percent. Local realtors are predicting two more years of downturn. Who would have predicted that the new projects of Widow Connection would count twenty-five widows as tailoring graduates in Africa? But that's hindsight.

What do we expect the year ahead to be like? Let's give that some thought. Is our behavior building for new possibilities? Are we managing the resources God has entrusted to us to move in a new direction? Are we open to doing new and different things unrelated to what we did in the past?

Remember Einstein's definition of insanity: doing the same thing and expecting different results. If you want a daily prompter, read one chapter of Proverbs every day this month. After reading each chapter, journal the most important piece of advice that applies to you today in your new life. Put that advice into practice. In one year you'll see the difference wisdom has made.

You won't spend it if . . . you are focused on your loss and the what-ifs, why-nots, and why-mes of your situation. Remember from chapter two, you can't have IT back. Determine to stop the two steps back for every three steps forward. That season is past, unless you choose to stay there.

Here's the test question for this one. How much time do you spend thinking about the past and those former dreams? You won't enjoy the next party or maybe even show up if you are still living as if your loss never happened.

You won't spend it if . . . you don't admit you have Kingdom Equity. I hope you fully embraced what we explored in chapter two. Ephesians 2:10 says, "For we are his workmanship, created in Christ Jesus for good works, which God afore prepared that we should walk in them" (ASV).

You are His workmanship, His masterpiece. You were chosen for the challenge. He built your back to be more than adequate for your burden. And you're still here. In other words, you're here on purpose.

You won't spend it if . . . you are filling those voids with hibernation, hoarding, and the other things we talked about in chapter three. Your life will be so cluttered with these ineffective attempts to fill the void that there will be no room to dance. A new party will simply be out of the question.

You won't spend it if . . . you see only the "trials and troubles" rather than the gifts you received during and after as a result of your loss. The temptations we talked about in chapter three will seem a good way to tread water if we are not looking at what we've gained.

These words from James contain echoes of all we've been learning in this book: "Consider it pure joy, my brothers, whenever you face trials of many kinds, because you know that the testing of your faith develops perseverance. Perseverance must finish its work so that you may be mature and complete, not lacking anything. If any of you lacks wisdom, he should ask God, who gives generously to all without finding fault, and it will be given to him" (James 1:2–5 NIV 1984). *Perseverance* is just another word for becoming the king or queen of "won't take no for an answer." "Mature, complete, and lacking nothing" is an excellent renaming of "simple, pared down, and satisfied." And wisdom can be described as discovering the good that has resulted from all the hard stuff that has gone before.

You won't spend it if . . . you don't accept that you are here and in this place on purpose. One new piece of equity He has invested in you is your ability to comfort others. You now know what it takes and how to do it. Second Corinthians 1:3–4 says, "Praise be to the God and Father of our Lord Jesus Christ, the Father of compassion and the God of all comfort, who comforts us in all our troubles, so that we can comfort those in any trouble with the comfort we ourselves have received from God."

Matthew 25 contains a story Jesus told of a wealthy man who went on a journey. He gave three men wealth to use while he was gone. One man received five bags of gold, one two, and one received one bag of gold. In his absence both the five-bag and the two-bag recipients doubled their investments. The one-bag recipient "hid his shoe box under the mattress," in a sense, and gained nothing. Read the story and note the rewards. You possess this Kingdom Equity on purpose.

You won't spend it if . . . you're stuck with bitterness without forgiving those in your past. Remember that the Before House and the Next House must be connected by forgiveness in your Now House. The word *thanksgiving* appears thirty times in the Bible. *Thanks* appears an additional seventy times. That means we should take notice! Thankfulness is important in our faith walk! What's the connection? It's difficult to be thankful when you're angry at someone. It's difficult to be thankful when you're nursing a wound and rehashing who or what caused it. In short, there's an important connection between forgiveness and thankfulness. I hope you've accomplished those all-important acts of forgiveness. Forgiveness almost always ushers us into being thankful. Being thankful is a huge chunk of equity.

Forgiving an offense, even when, in fact especially when, forgiveness has not been asked for opens our hearts to thanksgiving. Forgiveness and thanksgiving free us to spend our Kingdom Equity.

You Will Spend It If . . .

You will spend it if . . . you're ready for an adventure that is different from anything you've experienced before.

You will spend it if . . . you've decided what you value today and are willing to invest everything you have and are in that.

WILLING TO ADVENTURE

Let's describe what our adventurous new party might be.

Our new party can be described with some things we'd all like: new habits, vigor, a thankful spirit, peace of mind, and a healthy body. All of those aren't guaranteed, but our own choices after loss can make each of them more likely.

The party ahead must be different because our world has been changed. We don't need to think of adventure as doing wild and crazy things. Adventure can simply mean something different, exposure to new people and experiences in the new life. The book of Ruth in the Old Testament describes three women who all experienced loss. In this case, each of them lost a husband. Each of the three responded in a quite different way. Ferree Hardy points out in her excellent book, *A Path for Widows*, that Orpah returns to her previous life, her "own" people, and the familiar past. We don't know, however, whether what she returned to as a young widow was as positive as she hoped. Naomi, being practical, returned to the familiar she knew, her old homeland with its expectations and the familiar sights and smells of her younger days. Ruth stepped into a totally new life with different foods to eat, different expectations, different smells, and new relatives. She became an immigrant. She turned her back on her past faith in the god Molach who demanded infant sacrifice. She embraced the faith she saw lived in the life of her tenacious mother-in-law. She embraced Jehovah.[23]

Ruth literally walked into the unknown, a five-day, hard journey, on foot: her own road to Bethlehem and her place of conversion. She is an outstanding example of choosing to be transformed rather than conformed to her past life. And the book in Scripture describing the lives of these women is named for her.

Being ready for a party different from anything you've ever experienced means you are ready to live with disruptive innovation. Remember that concept developed by Clayton Christensen? He beat heart attack, advanced stage cancer, and stroke—all in three years. His courageous attitude is admirable. But his real help to us was coining the new phrase "disruptive innovation." This concept can open our eyes to what we never imagined in the life we can live. He was describing business solutions where new simple technologies and inventions bring down big companies because what they do is no longer needed.

For example, cellular phones disrupted fixed line telephones. Community colleges are displacing four-year colleges. Discount retailers are displacing full-service department stores, and retail medical clinics, even the local drug stores are displacing traditional doctor's offices. (Where did you get your last flu shot?) Scanners have replaced duplicators. The list is long and interesting.

A recent disruptive innovation is a new tire design by Michelin. These new tires are airless. This means no more air valves, no more air compressors at gas stations, no more repair kits, and no more flat tires. This is all good news for Michelin. It is bad news for all those companies who make products we'll no longer need.

The concept of disruptive innovation has application for our lives after loss and tragedy. We can discover simple, unexpected solutions to the new challenges in our lives. The void can be filled with what we might not have imagined before. Our loss has been disruptive, without a doubt. But innovation would never have happened otherwise.

We have a choice. We are not forced to embrace opportunity. We can stagnate and not allow our minds room to explore new beginnings. We can keep our ditto machine that leaves us with blue fingers (most of you readers have never heard of this relic that we vintage educators used to make copies on). We can keep our landline phones and drive on tires that need air and therefore can be punctured on dark nights on bad roads. Or we can embrace new beginnings and the beauty that disruption has brought to our lives.

I never imagined myself hiking in beautiful places with like-minded adventurous women, traveling sometimes solo through Africa on a mission, or road-tripping with three grandsons to see our country's heritage-marking places. These innovative adventures could only happen after disruption to my life as it had been.

We can settle in to isolation and let our minds continually recycle, trying to wrap around the unthinkable. Living with a shriveled soul in hibernation is a choice we can make. Or we can embrace change and embrace the party of our new lives.

DECIDE WHAT YOU VALUE

As you plan to spend your Kingdom Equity, determine what purposes you might value enough to spend all you have and give all that's in you for that purpose.

That simple directive is not so easily lived. I struggled to decide what that purpose might be in my own life. A defining moment came a year after my husband's exit to heaven, when I attempted to create what would be our memorial marker. It was easy to create those words that described Bob. I simply had his favorite verses inscribed: "Trust in the LORD with all your heart and lean not on your own understanding; in all your ways submit to him, and he will make your paths straight" (Proverbs 3:5–6). Under that inscription would be the words, "He humbly served others." Humble service was so clearly the top value of Bob's life. It was crystal clear what he stood for, lived his life for, and what we remembered him for.

So? It made me wonder, Whatever on earth describes me? I shared a few ideas with my daughter. Maybe "She loved him," as caring for Bob had been such a central calling in my life. Or maybe simply, "She loved," which would include more of the people I valued. I even suggested that we just leave it blank for me, and folks could think whatever they wished! But my daughter rejected all those suggestions and stated plainly, "It needs to say, 'She laughed, she loved, she lived large.'" Valerie could see what I had not yet seen for myself: what aspects of my life and experience would continue to define me in my future. And, yes, it does describe my new party.

In thinking what tops your value list, think of how you'd like to be remembered. *Legacy* seems like a stiff word, something beyond what most of us can aspire to. But it's not. We will leave an imprint on those whose lives we've touched. What do you and I want that imprint to be?

Look at your checkbook or online banking activity. Mine shows that I value interesting experiences with others more than giving things. Taking family members to Africa, letting life drop in memorable moments in unusual places is something I treasure. Boating on different lakes exploring cliffs and bluffs from the view on the water ranks high in what opens my wallet and finds its way into my crowded calendar.

Many are deciding that renting that big house on the water's edge and bringing in all the family may be a better onetime lifetime legacy than any annual gift giving. In order to afford the location, meals may have to be inexpensive (macaroni and cheese as the staple food), but it might be well worth it. Do you remember a material gift someone gave you ten years ago? Probably not. But what is in your memory bank? Likely there are valuable gifts of time spent together stored there.

As for me, education for grandchildren is another. What better investment than in their future? Big gift expenses of things at birthday time and Christmas don't appeal to me so much.

My friend Kathleen Rehl has modified a great tool that can help sort out what matters to you. Sharpen your pencil and let this exercise sharpen your focus on your most important values.[24]

RATING YOUR LIFE VALUES

This exercise will help you think about what you value most in your life. Here are sixteen key values that people often claim. Some say they want more of these values than others. You cannot realize them all because one may contradict another.

Assume you have to give up eleven of these values. Which would they be? Remove them by putting an "X" in the left column. Finally, rank your top five remaining value preferences, from highest (1) to lowest (5).

ACHIEVEMENT

_____ Accomplish something important in life:
be involved in significant activities;
succeed at what I am doing.

ADVENTURE

_____ Experience variety and excitement;
respond to challenging opportunities.

AESTHETICS

_____ Appreciate and enjoy beauty for beauty's sake;
be artistically creative.

AUTHORITY/POWER

_____ Be a key decision maker, directing priorities,
activities of others, and/or use of resources.

AUTONOMY

_____ Be independent, have freedom,
live where I want to be and do what I want to do.

GENEROSITY

_____ Give time and/or money to benefit others;
express gratitude for blessings in life.

HEALTH

_____ Be physically, mentally, and emotionally well;
feel energetic and have a sense of well-being.

INTEGRITY

_____ Be honest and straightforward, just and fair.

INTIMACY/FRIENDSHIP/LOVE

_____ Have close personal relationships, experience affection,
share life with family and friends.

PLEASURE

_____ Experience enjoyment and
personal satisfaction from my activities.

RECOGNITION

_____ Be seen as successful;
receive acknowledgment for achievements.

SECURITY

_____ Feel stable and comfortable with
few changes or anxieties in my life.

SERVICE

_____ Contribute to the quality of other people's lives
and help to improve society or the world.

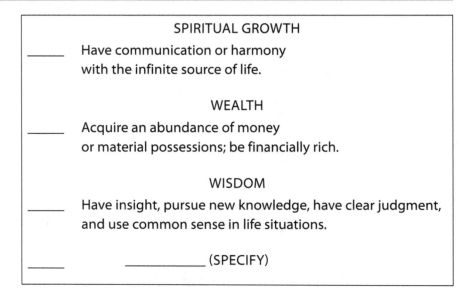

SPIRITUAL GROWTH

_____ Have communication or harmony
with the infinite source of life.

WEALTH

_____ Acquire an abundance of money
or material possessions; be financially rich.

WISDOM

_____ Have insight, pursue new knowledge, have clear judgment,
and use common sense in life situations.

_____   _____ (SPECIFY)

YOUR LIST

Those values you have identified will be the engine fueling and providing the passion for your season of spending your equity. So make your list. What equity do you have? It's not a job résumé. Yes, work skills and experiences might be on that list. But you are much more than the jobs you've had. What unusual experiences have you had? What have you learned from mentors? Whether you have ever been able to use what you learned is not the issue. It may just be that the prime opportunity is yet ahead in your future.

Ask friends who know you well to identify what equity they see in your life.

Think about new skills you don't have now but you'd like to have. Now that you've determined your values and what you want to invest in, what equipping do you need in order to accomplish those values and investments?

In the season of my daughter's loss, when she was facing the imminent death of her father, she decided to embark on earning a law degree. With three grade-school sons and a traveling husband, the timing seemed unlikely—unless you understood her desire to spend her Kingdom Equity and let no experience be wasted.

Embarking on new careers that require retooling your skill box is a frequent item on our equity list.

Many who are recovering from substance abuse want to invest their wisdom in those struggling on the same journey. While some become sponsors, others complete professional training and become professional counselors. They gained some Kingdom Equity and decided to add more.

Your list is not a static list. Your equity will grow as you use it. Leave room to add more. Here's one more assignment before we move on.

Take a bold marker and write across your list *How will I spend it?*

I referred earlier to one of my favorite statements by Martin Luther: "God can make one so desperately bold!" Spending our Kingdom Equity definitely requires that desperate boldness. In the aftermath of 9/11 we've seen examples of people who experienced the taste of grief but did not waste that grief. Most of us have moved on, seldom noticing our changed lives. We're annoyed at the airport over invasive search procedures, but we move on.

Many families who lost a dad or daughter in the tragedy have moved, literally. One mom moved her family of six—three biological children and one adopted child at the time of the Twin Towers disaster, and two adopted afterward. She didn't want the constant reminders and questions that might keep her family facing backward. A life of moving on? Hardly. But moving for sure. Her family tree was severely shaken, and her children have struggled. They count themselves rich to have added two more children to their tree. Many of those 9/11 stories truly represent beauty coming from ashes. The fire-creating ashes that took that daddy's life was the refining heat that motivated that mother to adopt two more children. We are beginning to see the long-term effects of tragedy.

On 9/11, the immediate news was all loss, all terrifying. But consider the beauty that's beginning to show. One lawyer took a 70 percent pay cut to move across the country and coach gymnastics. One publishing executive became an ordained pastor and adopted a child. And these are but a few of the more visible stories of lives changed.

Tragedy by another definition is disruptive innovation. What do these courageous people demonstrate? That they are spending their Kingdom

Equity on people. Things have become so much less important. An address, a professional title, an inscription on an office door—even having an office door—these lose significance when we spend our Kingdom Equity.

 Tragedy by another definition is disruptive innovation.

There is one investment that has become uncommon. It is valuable. As you look for ways to spend your Kingdom Equity, I hope this becomes something you do in great measure. In fact, I hope it becomes a habit. Spend some of your equity showing gratitude.

A journalist recently reported this story. Typically Chicago weather is fickle. A steady downpour descended suddenly on the Loop at rush hour, sending crowds scurrying for the elegant, historic entryway of a Chicago hotel, the Palmer House. The doorman there could hail them a cab and escort them under his umbrella into that cab. They would be dry. The doorman? He was pretty drenched by the thirtieth customer. That thirtieth person was our journalist. He had noticed that not one of these folks had tipped the doorman. He asked the doorman if it bothered him. Patrick Henry politely answered, "Perhaps they just don't understand, sir. Perhaps they just don't know." This gentleman protected the guests. He followed, "I approach every day the same. I'm glad to have my job." His income is a fraction of most of those for whom he hailed a cab that drenching evening downpour.

So how hard is it to have a few bills handy that can be retrieved even on a rainy night? The difference between a 15 percent and 20 percent tip in a restaurant is small. But it sends a big message to that person who has been on his or her feet trying to please an incredible variety of customers and probably has a less-than-perfect life outside that job.

Gratitude often does not involve money. It's that "Thank you" that takes longer than two seconds in which you expand on why you are saying those easy words.

Thank the postal worker in your post office and wish him or her a good day.

I have often been inspired by Jill Briscoe, who, in my view, has been spending her Kingdom Equity well. A gifted Bible teacher, artist, communicator, Jill has traveled the world to teach—sometimes in places where her life and that of her husband, Stuart, would have been in jeopardy had authorities known that they were Christians who were teaching the Bible.

I drank in Jill's wisdom and courage at an event. She was past seventy years of age and had just come back from a multi-week teaching time in a closed country. Her message to us was, "Go where you're sent, stay where you're put, and give what you've got." Jill's message may have a missionary sound, but it also applies to us as we embrace our new party.

We may have been sent here by circumstances, or our own behavior that created our loss. Whether chosen or sent, we're here. Rather than staying where we're sent in the sense of being stuck, stay in the place rather than running from reality and learn what we need to learn. And then move up and out; open the door to your Next House. A big part of loving this new party (the one you never dreamed you'd have) is giving what you've got.

Spend your Kingdom Equity.

Acknowledgments

Should an author admit that a book was not her idea? I must, because it's the truth. Nancy Hamlin, my new friend and grief support workshop leader and teacher at Willow Creek Community Church, suggested I write this with reasons so compelling that the only answer could be "Yes."

"Just a thought," Nancy said. "Have you ever considered doing a book not directed *solely* at widows? So much of what you have to say is important to all of us. You have such great, God-inspired, practical advice for surviving a loss. Just a thought."

I saw myself muddling through unwanted changes. Nancy saw more. Thank you, Nancy.

Then I had a "chance encounter" with Greg Thornton, senior vice-president of media at Moody Bible Institute. We were both hurrying through the halls between meetings at the Religious Broadcasters Convention. Greg expressed interest in seeing the proposal! How green can the light be? The only thing left to do was start writing. Thank you, Greg.

Figuring out where to go after the long list of losses and unexpected changes in my life was a necessity. But living **boldly**? That part was optional. However, my personal cheering section left me no choice but to move ahead.

Encouraging children and their spouses listened to my reasons why bold actions were not my style. Simply and quietly, their eyes told me, "We expect you to act"; they knew that "no" was not my final answer. Thank you, my loving family.

And then there is the example of my grandsons—bold-living grandsons who demonstrated that not knowing the outcome does not allow you to be fearful or permit inaction. The three of you entered our family during a rugged time of loss. Each of you had already experienced so many goodbyes in your short lives. And quickly you were saying another goodbye to a really good grandpa.

Albert, you were six the day we first met you—when you stepped in our door, looked up at your new grandpa and then down at his big puffy Indiana University house slippers. You looked up into his face with a broad grin. He matched that. You were his first grandson; it was a connection he treasured. He couldn't run with you long enough and certainly could not match your speed if he were with us today. But if he could see you, your resilience and determination (especially on display on the wrestling mat), his smile would be bigger than ever.

Edward, with your scientific, technical, fix-it inclination, you became your grandpa's hands and feet as ALS took his mobility. The two of you pored over instructions as you assembled things for him. Logical minds in harmony, both of you with quiet, understated talent, both with quick wit. He loved the sound of your laughter. He wouldn't be surprised that today you're researching robots for the sheer pleasure of it. He'd be cheering you on.

Edmond, our youngest grandson, you told your soccer coach that you did not have a grandpa long enough. How true! Even at age seven, you could recognize a man of character and wanted more of him in your life. Perhaps character recognizes character. I've watched your athletic talent on full display in football, wrestling, and rugby. As great as that talent is, it's a distant second to your character on display. If Grandpa were on your sidelines, the two of you would make eye contact and he'd give you his nodding approval.

In the days before your grandpa left us for heaven, I remember him telling each of you that he was sad not to be here to see the fine young men you would become. Now that you are seventeen, seventeen, and sixteen, your little boyhood is over. You have become men. And he'd be proud.

Why am I living boldly today? You inspire me because you keep stepping up to the harder challenges in life, you take the difficult academic path, and compete in the toughest of sports like wrestling, rugby, football, and soccer. I see your character especially in those moments when life is not fair. Rather than impulse at the moment, I see restraint, self-control, and good choices that invest for your future.

My new, bold living—sailing solo on a catamaran on the ocean, cliff jumping, Africa travels to help the disadvantaged—runs on our synergy. You set the example high and inspire me to live large.

Thank you to each of you who see more than I see and have greater courage than I. *Bold* is better, delightful and fun, meaningful, and it matches God's plan for each of us.

Study Guide

CHAPTER ONE:
THE BIGGEST LOSER IS . . .

1. Have you taken time to actually make a list of your "What If?" questions? This worthwhile exercise can be an important step in your new beginning. Then, if you're able to crumple up the list and throw it away, do so with great gusto!

2. Are there people you notice now who were invisible to you before? How has your loss opened your eyes to others?

3. Answer these questions to help you decide what to do with *things* after loss:

   Question # 1: To whom does this belong?
   Question # 2: What is the optimal time to decide for you, given your circumstance?
   Question # 3: What is the true emotional quotient of that thing?
   Question # 4: Does this thing represent, in a good way, my new life?
   Question # 5: Where is a good landing place for this thing?

CHAPTER TWO:
YOU CAN'T HAVE IT BACK

"Facts are stubborn things." *John Adams*

1. If you seem stuck in negative memories and regrets and are having trouble moving forward, jot a list of the main issues that trouble you, then look at your list with the perspectives we covered about acceptance.

2. Consider which of the events of the past simply were not in your control. This should make it easier for you to let them go.

3. Which items could be written over with the words, "Regrettable and now forgettable"? Only perfect people have no regrets.

4. Can you look at your past and see some events that helped prepare your back for this burden? What were some strengths from your past that can help you today?

5. Can you begin to glimpse what might happen as you become mustard-seed strong? Given the strength you are beginning to experience, what are some positive changes you'd like to consider?

6. What situation in your life today is your "But God" moment? Imagine how He might see this. Ask Him to show you what you should be thinking. Does the Bible have instruction related to your situation?

CHAPTER THREE:
TEMPTATIONS: FILLING THE VOID

"What lies behind us and what lies in front of us are but tiny matters as compared to what lies within us." *Ralph Waldo Emerson*

1. After reading about these temptations, rate them from 1 to 5, with 1

being the temptation to which you are most vulnerable and 5 being the temptation to which you are least vulnerable:

Hoarding: spending and keeping

Handing out: giving to get something back

Hunger: food or relationships: wrong person, time, or reason

Hiding: stepping back from life or pretending

Hibernation: let no one come into my space again

2. What boundaries could you put in place to reduce your vulnerability?

3. Ask yourself the following questions:

Hoarding: Are the costs and bills of what I am accumulating beyond what my budget can accommodate?

Handing out: Do I give with an expectation of something I want back in return?

Hunger: How long will the solution I'm using be effective? (This answer depends on whether we fill the void with a healthy, satisfying solution.) Am I filling that connection void with the wrong person, for the wrong reason, or at the wrong time?

Hiding: Is my hiding a place of healing or avoidance? Are my thoughts continually turning backward, mulling over the past? Is the space around me deteriorating in care and appearance? Am I taking care of my body? Is this temporary hiding period potentially good? Am I investing time in thinking about the future? Am I regularly in contact with someone who has my best interests at heart?

Hibernation: Have I invited someone into my space, to get a fresh set of eyes who might see my hiding is becoming a place of hibernation?

4. A time of loss is a time when we are vulnerable to filling that void with wrong relationships, at the wrong time, or for the wrong reasons. The following chart will help you determine if the influencing people around you are wise or foolish.[25]

FACTS ABOUT FOOLS	**FACTS ABOUT WISE PEOPLE (WP)**
Fools exist.	Wise people exist.
We don't identify fools. Matthew 5:21–23	Any person can become a wise person. Proverbs 2:1–11
Fools identify themselves. Proverbs 12:23	WP identify themselves by their actions. Proverbs 3:13–18
God identifies fools. Proverbs 1:7	God identifies wise people. Proverbs 3:13–18
A fool will not be reconciled. Proverbs 20:3, 29:9	A WP seeks reconciliation. Proverbs 19:11; Romans 12:18
A fool is always right. Proverbs 12:15	A WP knows she is imperfect. Proverbs 2:1–5, 20:9
A fool trusts herself. Proverbs 1:32, 28:26	A WP trusts God, not herself. Proverbs 2:6–11
A fool doesn't think straight. Proverbs 18:2, 22:3	A WP thinks straight. Romans 12:1–3
A fool repeats her folly. Proverbs 26:11, 27:12	A WP learns from her failure. Psalm 119:65–68
A fool reveals only her own opinion. Proverbs 18:2	A WP seeks God's mind. Psalm 119:45–48
A fool does not listen. Proverbs 1:22–32	A WP listens. Proverbs 1:33
A fool does not think. Proverbs 14:16	A WP thinks. Proverbs 4:26–27
A fool does not learn. Proverbs 17:10	A WP learns. Psalm 119:105, 124–125
A fool believes there is no God. Psalm 53:1	A WP knows God IS and guides. Psalm 121:1–4
A fool wrecks herself/blames God. Proverbs 19:3	A WP accepts responsibility. Proverbs 19:21; Romans 14:12

5. As we spend time with a person, we can ask ourselves evaluating questions about the person's behavior in each of these eleven areas. Some are easy to answer from just talking and hanging out. Others take a little more time, perception, and observation.

Is she/he "at odds" with many people from her past as well as present?

Does she/he communicate "my way or the highway"?

Does his/her behavior reflect biblical instruction and guidance?

Does he/she have the uncommon quality of common sense?

Does he/she repeat unhealthy patterns and unwise choices (i.e., stays in debt, stays in destructive relationships, repeatedly lacks self care)?

Is she/he self-absorbed? Does she strive to monopolize your calendar?

Does he/she monopolize conversations? Does he selectively listen to others including you?

Do you find yourself doing mental gymnastics trying to understand her/his statements, reasoning, or beliefs?

Does he/she seem to get stuck in unwise situations and relationships either with an inability to see what's real or the unwillingness to act on what's real?

Does her/his speech and behavior mirror her belief in God and desire to humbly attempt to live likewise?

Are his/her problems always someone else's fault, including God's?

6. How can we tell we are vulnerable to becoming involved in friendships not in our best interests? When we *excuse behavior* in the foolish category, we are vulnerable. When we accept/tolerate behavior not in our best interests, we are vulnerable. Often before we recognize the behavior, we sense an uncomfortable feeling.

Do you feel emotionally and even physically drained just being around a person? That is a warning flag.

Do you find yourself rationalizing his/her behavior?

She/he says . . . and promises future behavior that will be different from what you are seeing now. ("I'll be paying off that maxed credit card when I get my raise in three months" or "I'll be able to call you more often when this work project is done.")

7. Remember: Behavior never lies. If you've read these lists and still can not determine if this person you were in a relationship with before was wise or foolish, make two lists. What BEHAVIOR did you observe that you can write under a "Wise" list? What BEHAVIOR did you observe that you can write under a "Fool" list? Let those actions speak.

8. Avoid the temptation to rationalize another person's poor behavior by past circumstances:
   "He/she does that because . . ."

9. Avoid the temptation to excuse another person's poor behavior because of your own poor behavior: "I'm partly to blame because . . ." The I'm-Partly-to-Blame Syndrome has a two-part solution.
   1) Make sure your own behavior is straight and not squishy, then see if the other person's behavior changes.
   2) Don't accept blame inappropriately to help someone else look better.

10. Start investing your resources. In what settings do you grow well? This is a good time to consider your dreams. When you were a young adult, what prompted you to study the extra hour, run the extra mile? What were your passions and the desires of your heart?

CHAPTER FOUR:
BETTER: THE BLUE BOWL PERSPECTIVE

1. Sketch your boardroom table. Draw at least six stick chairs around it. You need not be an artist to do this. And no one else needs to see your drawing. Consider who you want to invite to sit in each of these chairs. Choose your Board of Directors:

A godly person who has experienced a similar loss:

"Praise be to the God and Father of our Lord Jesus Christ, the
Father of compassion and the God of all comfort, who comforts
us in all our troubles, so that we can comfort those in any trouble
with the comfort we ourselves receive from God"
(2 Corinthians 1:3–4).

"By wisdom a house is built, and through understanding it is estab-
lished; through knowledge its rooms are filled with rare and
beautiful treasures" (Proverbs 24:3–4).

A person with financial wisdom:

"Honor the Lord with your wealth, with the firstfruits of all your
crops" (Proverbs 3:9).

"The earth is the Lord's, and everything in it, the world, and all who
live in it" (Psalm 24:1).

"Let no debt remain outstanding, except the continuing debt to love
one another, for whoever loves others has fulfilled the law"
(Romans 13:8).

A practical friend:

"Plans fail for lack of counsel, but with many advisers they succeed"
(Proverbs 15:22).

"For the Lord will be your confidence and will keep your foot from
being snared" (Proverbs 3:26 NIV 1984).

An encourager:

"Finally, brothers, whatever is true, whatever is noble, whatever is
right, whatever is pure, whatever is lovely, whatever is
admirable—if anything is excellent or praiseworthy—think
about such things. Whatever you have learned or received or
heard from me, or seen in me—put it into practice. And the
God of peace will be with you" (Philippians 4:8–9 NIV 1984).

A person with spiritual discernment & courage:

> "As iron sharpens iron, so one person sharpens another" (Proverbs
> 27:17).

A relative whose priority is YOUR well-being:

> "A man of many companions may come to ruin, but there is a friend
> who sticks closer than a brother" (Proverbs 18:24 NIV 1984).

2. Write the names of people you would like in each chair. They may be
   helpful people in your current circle, or you may need to reach out and
   connect more intentionally with a person whose wisdom you need.
   Remember, through books and other resources, you have access to the
   wisdom of people from previous generations and faraway locations.

3. Turn your attention to filling your Big Blue Bowl. What do you most
   need in it?

4. What life structures might you change in order to be transformed?
   Write them down and add them to your Blue Bowl.

5. Consider what you feed your body. Write that new list for your BB.

6. Consider what you feed your soul. What is your new resolve to feed
   your soul? Put that list in your BB.

7. Consider and evaluate those people in whom you invest your time. List
   the people changes you need to make. Add that to your BB.

8. One of the most important lists is your gratitude list. At least, put a
   starter list in your BB.

CHAPTER FIVE:
FORGIVENESS: MORE THAN
RECOMMENDED, IT'S REQUIRED

1. Have you made a list of those you believe have wronged you or participated in your loss? I know it's a hard assignment and is emotionally
draining to review. But the reward in the long run will be worth it.

2. Are there people with whom you might make amends? In summary,
here are those steps from Matthew 18:15–17.
    First, talk with the person.
    If there's no resolution, bring in another person.
    If reconciliation was not successful, we are to distance ourselves
        from that person.
    If reconciliation is impossible, we need to learn to move on, given
        that reality.

3. Take a piece of paper and fold it in thirds. Above the left third write *Before
House*; above the right third, write *Next House*; and above the middle
third, write *Now House*. Write or sketch anything that comes to mind in
each section. Make sure the middle section includes forgiveness.

CHAPTER SIX:
THE PARTY YOU (DIDN'T KNOW YOU) WANTED

"God can make one so desperately bold!" *Martin Luther*
The hottest fires make the hardest steel.

1. Maslow's hierarchy of needs and its influence can be negative. It can be
helpful to compare this perspective from psychology, which is human-
istic and individualistic, to the biblical perspective of our needs.

2. Abraham Maslow's hierarchy of needs supposedly described the stages
of growth in humans. His pyramid assumes that needs at the bottom of
the pyramid must be satisfied before the most desirable goals at the top
become a reality.

Self-actualization:	reaching one's full potential, becoming all we can be; based on mastering all the previous needs
Esteem:	acceptance and value by others, self-esteem and self-respect gained through recognition
Love and Belonging:	a sense of belonging and being loved usually met through friendship, intimacy, and family
Safety needs:	physical safety and economic safety: physical safety and lack of harm and economic security
Physiological needs:	literal requirements for human survival such as air, water, food, and shelter

3. Contrast that with a biblical perspective. Here's what Scripture says about:

Self-actualization: "Not so with you. Instead, whoever wants to become great among you must be your servant" (Matthew 20:26).

Esteem: "But godliness with contentment is great gain. For we brought nothing into the world, and we can take nothing out of it. But if we have food and clothing, we will be content with that" (1 Timothy 6:6–8).

Love and Belonging: "And my God will meet all your needs according to the riches of his glory in Christ Jesus" (Philippians 4:19).

Safety needs: "I am not saying this because I am in need, for I have learned to be content whatever the circumstances" (Philippians 4:11).

Physiological needs: "I know what it is to be in need, and I know what it is to have plenty. I have learned the secret of being content in any and every situation, whether well fed or hungry, whether living in plenty or in want" (Philippians 4:12).

4. Make a list of the equity built into you through experiences, skills, and even personality characteristics. Ask friends who know you well what equity they see in you.

5. As you rate your values, reflect on whether the way you use money reflects what you truly value. See the chart on pages 148–150 to help you clarify those values.

6. Put your money where your values are. Money can be a means to an end, not just the end itself. When you use your money in ways that reflect your true values, you'll probably feel happier, too. Describe a time when you felt good about spending money in a way that matched your values. Have you ever spent money in a way that didn't support your values? If so, describe that incident. Look at your number one top value. What's one way you can use some of your money to align with this important value?

7. Remember that you are rich in Kingdom Equity, God's investment in you. Events, whether positive or negative, have gifted you with wisdom, experience, information, and faith. Everything in your life is a part of God building equity, a valuable investment. How will you spend it?

Notes

1. Realty Trac, "U.S. Foreclosure Trends and Foreclosure Market Statistics," National Real Estate Trends, August 25, 2011. www.realtytrac.com/trendcenter.

2. Andy Andrews, *The Butterfly Effect* (Naperville, IL: Simple Truths, LLC, 2009).

3. Leif Lundblad, quoted in Andrew Ward, "ATM Pioneer Looks to Change Banking Again," *The Financial Times*, May 17, 2011. www.ft.com.

4. Patricia Reaney, "Poll: Belief in Supreme Being Strong Across Globe," FaithWorld, April 29, 2011. www.reuters.com.

5. zapsizzleboom.com, September 13, 2011.

6. Wikipedia.com.

7. Ben Summerskill, "Shopping Can Make You Depressed," *The Observer*, May 5, 2001. www.guardian.co.uk.

8. Henry Cloud, *Necessary Endings* (New York: HarperCollins, 2010).

9. Jan Silvious, *Foolproofing Your Life* (Colorado Springs, CO: WaterBrook Press, 1998).

10. Warren Zevon song title "Lawyer, Guns and Money," quoted in Cloud, *Necessary Endings*.

11. Paraphrased from this complete quote from J. Hudson Taylor: "I have found there are three stages to every great work of God: first it is impossible, then it is difficult, then it is done."

12. Jerry Sittser, *A Grace Disguised: How the Soul Grows Through Loss* (Grand Rapids: Zondervan, 2004).

13. Definition adapted from Florence Denmark, et al., "Forgiveness: A Sampling of Research Results," American Psychological Association. www.apa.org.

14. Definition from the Oxford English Dictionary, accessed online.

15. C. Van Oyen, et al., "Granting Forgiveness or Harboring Grudges: Implications for Emotions, Physiology and Health," *Psychological Science*, 12 (2001), 117–23.

16. S. Sarinopoulos, "Forgiveness and Physical Health: A Doctoral Dissertation Summary," *World of Forgiveness*, 2 (2000), 16–18.

17. Fred Luskin, Ph.D., *Forgive for Good: A Proven Prescription for Health and Happiness* (New York: Harper, 2002).

18. Ibid.

19. Miriam Neff, "A New Faith," *From One Widow to Another* (Chicago: Moody Publishers, 2009), chapter 10.

20. Cloud, *Necessary Endings*.

21. Ibid.

22. Chart appears under "Maslow's Hierarchy of Needs" at www.wikipedia.org.

23. Ferree Hardy, *A Path for Widows*, self-published. See www.widowschristianplace.com.

24. Thanks to Ken Rouse for his kind permission to adapt this exercise from life values information in his book *Putting Money In Its Place* (Dubuque, IA: Hunt Publishing Co., 1994).

25. Jan Silvious, *Foolproofing Your Life* (Colorado Springs, CO: WaterBrook Press, 1998).